# The 100 Most Beautiful

# in English

## Robert Beard

(Dr. Goodword at alphaDictionary)

# Lexiteria

Lexiteria LLC
Lewisburg, Pennsylvania 17837

Library of Congress Control Number: 2009907715

**Published by Lexiteria LLC**
Lewisburg, Pennsylvania
August 2009
ISBN-13: 978-0-9841723-0-6

*to Greg*

*for a half century of love and friendship*

*and the journey of a life time*

# Contents

# Acknowledgements

Over the past ten years at *yourDictionary.com* and *alphaDictionary.com* I have received thousands of suggestions for words to write up in my word-of-the-day series. Many have been accompanied by suggestions of content, issues to address, and reasons for the suggestions. Many of the words in this book, and in my previous book, *The 100 Funniest Words in English*, were suggested either directly by e-mail or in one of the forums in our elite word discussion group at the *Alpha Agora*.

I would like to take this opportunity to thank those whose suggestions have led to Good Words in our daily word mailings. They include Riutaro Aida, "Apoclima" of the *Alpha Agora*, Luis Alejandro Apiolaza, Jan Arps, Eric Berntson, Chris Berry, Larry Brady, Katy Brezger, Colin Burt, Jeremy Busch, Christine Casalini, Rodger Collins, Stan Davis, James Dirks, Perry Dror, Cathy Hilborn Feng, Robert Fitzgerald, Susan Gold, "Grogie" of the *Alpha Agora*, John Hall, Morty and Evelyn Hershman, Brian Johnson, Lew Jury, Samuel Keays, Lyn Laboriel, Susan Lister, Kathleen McCune of Norway, Kyle McDonald, Michael Oberndorf, Paul Ogden, Luciano Eduardo de Oliveira, Brock Putnam, Gail Rallens, Norman and Phyllis Rich, Chris Stewart, Mary Jane Stoneburg, Jackie Strauss, Margie Sved, Gianni Tamburini, Cat Waters, Ann Walper, and Suzanne Williams.

I would like to offer a special word of gratitude to four dear supporters who edited the manuscript in ways most excellent. Paul Ogden and Luciano Eduardo de Oliveira not only have suggested words for the *alphaDictionary* Good Word series over the five years of its existence, for several years now they have edited them for me gratis. Now they have also edited this book, joined in this endeavor by Dawn Shawley, friend and lexicographer at Lexiteria, and Susan Gold of Westtown School, a former student and now old friend. My deepest gratitude to all of them for their sharp eyes, their knowledge of English grammar and style, and their kindness.

# What Makes Words Beautiful?

## What Are Words?

At the most basic level, a word is a combination of linguistically coded sounds associated with one or more meanings. However, words are much more than that.

*Sound.* First, words are not only sounds but rhythm sets, for each word has an accented syllable that stands out from the unaccented ones. In fact, an English word may have a highly accented syllable, a less prominently accented syllable, an unaccented syllable, and a reduced syllable, that is, a syllable reduced to the schwa sound "uh." *Expedient*, for example, has a less prominently accented syllable, *ex-*, followed by an accented syllable, *ped-*, then an unaccented syllable *i-*, and, finally, a reduced syllable *-ent* pronounced [unt].

The result of this play of accentuation in English words is a specific rhythm that combines with the rhythms of other words in a sentence to produce the rhythmics of a musical line. As we speak, these rhythms combine with the undulations of the intonation of our voices that express emphasis, surprise, disbelief, questioning, and the like. The final product that emerges from our lips is something very close to music. In fact, in my essay on rhyming compounds at alphaDictionary.com, I argue that little fellows like *ding-dong, roly-poly, shilly-shally* are musical flukes and folderol we use simply to decorate and add pleasure to our conversations.

*Meaning.* So, on the sound side, words are complexly musical. On the semantic side, too, much more is at stake than a word's definition. The meaning of a word is not its definition. The linguistic term for the basic definition of a word is *denotation*, that specific thing in life to which a word refers. But *connotation* is often more important than denotation. The connotation of a word is the associations that swirl around it in our minds, things related that pop into our mind when we hear or utter a word, things that we feel more than know about that word.

For example, the denotation of the word *mother* is the female parent. Simple; also boring. But when we speak of our own mother, the word brings a host of images, memories, emotions, feelings of love, warmth, frustration, security or vulnerability too numerous to even suggest here, all of which vary dramatically from person to person.

In measuring their beauty, we should keep in mind that the words we weave into music are also fibers of our consciousness, of our individual lives. So, in choosing the one hundred words I think the most beautiful, I have also kept in mind each word's associations with the history and culture of the English-speaking peoples and how they intermingle with the lives of individual speakers.

*Combination.* Words may have pleasant sounds that evoke pleasant senses but to make the list of the most beautiful words in English we also have to keep in mind how the sound and meaning fit. The best example of sound-meaning fit is onomatopoeia, words that sound like their meaning, words like *meow*, *quack*, and *moo*. However, sounds and meanings fit in subtler ways, too. Before delving too far into this question, though, let's take a closer look at each of these aspects of words, one by one, to see how they bring words their beauty.

## The Music of Words

Linguistic sounds are made by blowing air from the lungs over the vocal cords, vibrating them, then through the vocal tract (throat, nose, tongue, teeth, and lips), which shapes the sounds produced by the vocal cords. Vowels are the sounds in language formed by shaping the vocal tract without interrupting the flow of air from the lungs. Consonants involve either stopping the flow of air (try pronouncing [p], [t], or [k] consciously) or restricting it in some way so as to produce a noise, as we do pronouncing [f], [s], [sh] and [ch]. (I use square brackets throughout this book to distinguish the sounds of English from the letters representing them; letters will be indicated by capital letters.) Vowels tend to be lovelier because they are shaped by the vocal "pipes" alone without obstructions.

The vowels [o] and [u] are pronounced by 'rounding' (puckering) the lips. They appear more frequently than others in lovelier words, perhaps because lips are so involved in expressing love. That does not mean, though, that other vowel sounds are precluded from glamorous words. English has one other pleasantly soft sound, the schwa or 'uh' sound. Whether accented or not, it can add much to a word's glow and flow. Whatever the vowels may be, expect words with high vowel content to figure prominently in the chapters that follow.

Some consonants are just as comely as vowels. Of all the English consonants, those known as sonorants, [r], [l], [m], and [n], are the most musical for, in many languages, they are vowels. In fact, we find these sounds pronounced as vowels in most dialects of English. In the United States, for example, the word *little* is pronounced [**li**-dl], with a vocalic [l]. The vowel sound is pronounced over the [l], not before it. *Worker* is similarly pronounced [**wr**-kr]. The [r] is simply the sound [uh] with the tongue curled slightly upward. Expect these consonants to play prominent roles in decorative vocabulary.

Hushes like [sh], [zh] (the middle consonant in *fusion* and *azure*), [s] and [z] are spirants, breezy reminders of rustling leaves, stony brooks, or forbidden food sizzling in the back of our weight-conscious imaginations. Hissing sounds can add beauty to words, depending on the other sounds in the word and its meaning. Spirants like ([th], [dh], [f], and [v]) are also very soft sounds and soft is far more beautiful than hard.

## Pleasant Meanings from Pleasant Memories

*Denotations*. Occasionally the denotation of a word alone has allure. Words like *love*, *lilt*, and *dulcet* have beautiful senses however they might be pronounced. The rounded vowels and [l]s in their pronunciation only build on the semantic beauty of these words. These words need nothing more to make this book.

Certainly, this aspect of verbal beauty varies from person to person, since different people associate varying degrees of pleasure with the basic sense(s) of a given word. But certain words, like those just mentioned, universally convey some degree of pleasure with their denotation.

*Connotations*. A word with a pleasurable denotation gains in beauty with pleasurable connotations, associations with objects and activities of delight in our lives. We enjoy words that engage pleasant associations, as the spelling of *chatoyant* is remindful of a pleasant chat with someone we are fond of. The sound of *mellifluous* suggests mellowness while its meaning implies to me, at least, the sweetness of honey and the buzzing of (undisturbed) little bees and the flowers they haunt. *Inglenook* suggests a snug cranny and, again to me, a glass of wine, while *bungalow* is associated with coziness and warmth, a retreat from a punishing world, a house that is small and very personal. Connotations are personal but we do share many of them.

## The Sound-Meaning Fit

Some sounds fit their meaning better than others. The best of the misfits were included in *The 100 Funniest Words in English*. Words like turdiform "thrush-like," *crapulence*, the discomfort from overeating, and *fartlek*, a physical exercise routine are so horribly mismatched that the result is funny.

Other words are simply onomatopoetic, imitations of the sounds they name. These words include *crack*, *thud*, *tinkle*, *hiss*, and *quack.* Some of these words with an inkling of their meaning in their sound are more attractive. *Tintinnabulation* suggests the bright tinkling of a bell while *opprobrium*, with its dark back vowels, connects us mentally with the dark sense of foreboding underlying its meaning. The lexical beauty of such words arises more from the appropriateness of the relationship between their sounds and meanings than from either the sound or meaning in particular.

## Why are So Many Beautiful English Words Borrowed?

While no one knows the exact percentage, well over 50 percent of the English vocabulary is borrowed from French alone. The invasion of William the Conqueror in 1066 initiated the Norman Period of English history and the Middle English period of the language. Religious, judicial, educational, and governmental institutions were conducted mostly in French over this period. Old English became the language of the lower classes. Thousands of French words were imported into English, a process that continued even after English reestablished itself again around 1300 as the by then very strongly French-influenced national language.

English doesn't simply borrow words from other languages, though; it plunders other languages for their lexical treasures like a shameless vocabulary pirate. As the British Empire encircled the globe in search of natural resources, the British colonialists scanned the treasures of foreign vocabularies for additions to the English lexicon. Chinese (*kowtow*), Japanese (*sushi*), Indonesian (*ketchup*), German (*blitzkrieg*), Hindi (*hut, thug*), Russian (*galoshes, blintzes*), Spanish (*hoosegow, sierra*), Portuguese (*fandango*), Norwegian (*sky*) Swedish (*ski, smorgasbord*), all the Native American languages, North and South (*muskrat, tomato, chili, avocado*), plus dozens if not hundreds more languages, have surrendered very significant portions of their word treasures to stoke the voracity of the English lexicon.

Now, does that mean that English contains only a few thousand truly English words? Hardly. Once English borrows a word like *chatoyant* (pronounced [shatoyā] in French), changing its meaning and pronunciation (English [shætoyunt]) along the way, the word is English. That French words come from a language associated with high culture (haute couture, haute cuisine, etc.) and epicurean sophistication does add to the luster and allure of its vocabulary, but once English speakers adopt them, they are English.

A certain exoticity comes with borrowed words. The distance between two cultures engenders a kind of romantic mystery. That is why so many mysteries and spy thrillers are set in such mysterious places as Marrakesh, Samara, Tashkent, and Istanbul. The very names of these places exude mystery and romance; the same mystery and romance often accompanies the borrowed word.

## A Touch of History, A Touch of Class

So what makes a genuinely English word attractive? Old fashioned words also wear a special kind of beauty, a comforting reassurance like that of a favorite shirt or well-worn shoes. Words like *becoming*, *wherewithal*, *erstwhile*, and *fetching* bring along with them a sense of simpler, more comfortable times past, of a quaintness we look on fondly, like the home of a favorite aunt or grandmother. They carry that warm sense of security and ease we get from things that belong to us. These connotations set them off from others. Here the distance is in time rather than space but it is still the sense of removal that adds elegance and grace to such words.

This doesn't mean that current native words are not beautiful: *love*, *lilt* and *offing* certainly are beautiful; other factors do enter the lexical beauty equation. However, just as the sense of cultural distance endears us to borrowed words, temporal distance in native words can be just as appealing.

## Personal Favorites

Beauty, of course, ultimately rests in the eye of the beholder, so the beauty in words is to a large extent personal. In the song "Maria" in *West Side Story*, Maria's suitor, Tony, asserts that *Maria* is "[t]he most beautiful sound I ever heard." Certainly different names have the same impact on other men. The final choice of words in this book had to be mine. I could not have written about the beauty others see in words even had I polled my readers of the past ten years for their favorites. However, I have carefully selected these words from my experience in using, exploring and studying them, particularly while writing and publishing poetry in the 1970s (which I still hope to publish as a volume some day).

Choosing the one hundred words I thought the most beautiful was not easy. I thought of others and found it quite difficult drawing the line between the most beautiful and the runners-up. Those considered for inclusion and reluctantly omitted include *ember, embrace, exude, flower,* and *beautiful* itself—this after actually including more than a hundred words in this collection. You will probably be disappointed that some of your favorites are not here but then that is to be expected given the personal nature of beauty and its perception. I simply hope that you enjoy the beauty of my selection and my explorations of them.

Before enjoying the words themselves, however, we will need a very brief survey of where the English language comes from and how it is related to other languages. That is next.

# Background

Before exploring the beauty of the English vocabulary, we need to know a bit about how it stands among the languages of Europe, from which it borrowed more than half its words.

English is a Germanic language, brought to the British Isles by Angles and Saxons around 500 AD from the northern coast of what is today Germany. The original people living in the British Isles, and in northern France as well, were Celts. Celts spoke languages from a different family of languages. It included the various dialects of Gaelic (Irish, Manx, Scottish and Welsh) and Breton, spoken in what is known as Brittany in France today.

French, Italian, Portuguese, and Spanish are Romance languages, so called because they are the remnants of the language spoken in the Roman Empire, Latin. Latin spoken in France became French, Latin spoken in Italy became Italian, and so on.

The Germanic, Celtic, and Romance languages all belong to a greater 'Indo-European' family. It is called this because most of the languages spoken in India and Europe belong to this family. All the languages in Europe except Finnish, Estonian, Turkish, Hungarian, and Basque are Indo-European. Indic languages such as Hindi, Urdu, Marathi, and several other languages spoken in India, belong to the same family.

Linguists have partially reconstructed the original Indo-European language, called 'Proto-Indo-European,' spoken somewhere north of India about 6000 years ago, from which the Indo-European languages may be traced. This is done by comparing words for the same thing in all these languages. For example, the word for "father" in Latin is *pater*, in Greek *pater*, Gothic *fadar*, and in Sanskrit, the ancient language from which modern Indian languages developed, *pitar*.

These are the oldest languages for which we have extensive written evidence. By comparing these words (the comparative method), scientists have explained the rules which operated over time to create the modern languages we have today.

Apparently, the original Proto-Indo-European language contained a word for "father" that was, roughly, *pater*. In the Germanic languages, however, over time, the [p] became [f]. This change is then verified by looking at other words in these languages, where we find more evidence of this rule, such as Latin *piscus* and English *fish*, Latin plago "I strike" and English *flog*. Hundreds of such rules have now been established, proving that all these languages are related, descended from one ancient parent or proto-language.

So why are there so many Indo-European languages today, you rightly ask. What happened over the past 6000 or so years is this. As the populace speaking Proto-Indo-European expanded, those farthest from speakers in the central area began pronouncing words slightly differently. The result was the development of accents, then dialects, dialects like those spoken in Australia, the United States, and the United Kingdom. At first everyone could understand each other, though speakers from one region sounded a bit funny to speakers from another.

As time continued to pass, however, these differences became very deep, to the point that mutual understanding became very difficult and, finally, impossible. At this point, the different dialects were different languages. The same process would then take place again, and again, and again. Languages broke up into dialects, dialects became languages, which soon had dialects, and so on and on until we had a wide array of languages across Europe and northern India, languages which now have spread around the world.

Keeping this in mind, let's now explore some very beautiful words in the English language.

# *Pronunciation Guide*

The pronunciation examples throughout this book will follow the patterns in this guide.

| Symbol | Example | Symbol | Example |
|---|---|---|---|
| ah | father, odd | l | let, sell |
| ai | hide | m | mother |
| aw | all, walk, caught | n | not (N see below) |
| ay | day | o | old, stow, though |
| æ | cab | oo | mood, prude |
| æw | cow, plough | oy | oil, boy |
| b | but | p | pen |
| ch | chin | r | road, wring, rhyme |
| d | dad | s | say, city |
| dh | the, either | sh | sheep, nation |
| e | egg | th | thin, thick |
| ee | eel, eat, deceit | t | tote |
| f | fond, phase, laugh | u, uh | about, but, Cuba |
| g | go, wagon | U | good, would |
| h | hat | v | very |
| hw | when | w | wet |
| i | it | y | yes, n[y]ew |
| k | key, cat, back | z | zoo, busy |
| j | jet, geology | zh | vision, azure |
| N | Nasalized vowel made by opening the nasal passage as in uh-huh [uhN-huhN] "yes." | | |

## NOTE BENE: Glossary

Although most of the linguistic terms used in this book are defined where first used, a glossary of them is included at the end of this book.

# Ailurophile ❧ *Noun*

**Pronunciation:** uh-**loor**-uh-fail

An **ailurophile** is a cat-lover or, better yet, a fancier of cats, since this is such a fancy word.

This word derives its beauty in part from its sound association with *allure*, another beautiful English word. *Cat-lover* and *cat-fancier* are ambiguous and not at all dignified enough for our soft and supple feline friends. This word is specific, excluding any affection for lions and tigers. The adjective is *ailurophilic* and the love of cats is *ailurophilia*. If you don't like cats or are afraid of them, you are an ailurophobe.

*Ailurophile* refers specifically to cat cats, not loose, spiteful women or cool jazz musicians: "The weekly meeting of ailurophiles at the civic center focused on the question of how best to convince your cat that you are boss." That doesn't mean we cannot use it playfully: "Well, I find her a bit catty and I'm not an ailurophile." Of course, dogs tend to be ailurophiles in the strictest of strict senses. But if your dog runs away from cats, he suffers from ailurophobia.

This beautiful word first appeared in print only around 1927. So a recent English-speaker connected Greek ailur-os "house cat" and phil-os "friendly, fond of" with an [o] and slipped it into English. Not much is known of the origin of *ailuros* but the compounding element phil- "love" was used widely by the Greeks, providing us a gold mine to borrow from, including tree-hugging dendrophiles, cheese-loving turophiles, wine-loving oenophiles, and many, many others. Of course, here in Pennsylvania we have Philadelphia, which would actually seem to be the city of love (*phil-*) brothers (*adelphos*) rather than the city of brotherly love.

# Assemblage ❧ *Noun*

**Pronunciation:** uh-**sem**-blij

An **assemblage** may be the act of assembling or the state of being assembled. More interestingly, however, an assemblage is a set of parts that go together, either parts designed to fit together or random pieces assembled in a work of art.

Words on -*age* are usually beautiful, especially if given the French pronunciation [ahzh]. In this word it has been Anglicized to [idj]. Still, the blend of the vowel-like M and L with the breezy S makes *assemblage* a very lovely word all the same. This is the noun from the verb *assemble*. It has a rather less appealing sister, *assembly*, whose meaning is more restricted, referring only to assemblages of people.

Like its sister, *assembly*, this word may refer to people: "Leslie's parties were always an assemblage of the most enlightened people in town." However, unlike *assembly*, it may refer to anything assembled from various components: "The bouquet was an assemblage of dried desert flowers Leslie had picked as she drove through the Nevada backcountry."

This lovely word came to English from Old French assembler "to assemble," a reduction of Vulgar Latin *assimulare* made up of the preposition ad "(up) to" + simul "at the same time, together." *Simul* also shows up in another time word, *simultaneous*. It is based on the primitive root sem- "one, all together" which also appears in many Indo-European words meaning "same," including *same* itself. In Greek, however, where an initial [s] often changes to [h], the word for "same" there is *homos*, which is found in many borrowed words intimating sameness in English, including *homogenize*, *homonym*, and *homotropic*.

# Becoming ❧ *Adjective*

**Pronunciation:** buh-**kum**-ing

The basic meaning of the adjective *becoming* is "attractive" but it may refer either to attractive people or attractive behavior (*behaviour* outside the US), where the meaning leans more toward "appropriate for the circumstances."

A very comely word, this. The two humming sounds, M and NG, lay the foundation for the beauty of this word. The B and the M are labial sounds, formed with the lips alone, and the association of the lips with affection and delicious tastes helps lift this word above the rest. *Becoming* originated as the present participle of the verb *become*, but in a quirky meaning which that verb bears, "to make attractive," as in, "That dress becomes you." You may use this word negatively if you properly prefix it, as in "behavior unbecoming an officer."

Remember the two senses of this word. It can refer to sheer physical beauty: "Natalie Cladd's broad-brimmed hat sat askew on her hair in a becoming fashion that no one could ignore." As a result, Natalie herself most likely cut a becoming figure. But this word may also refer to the appropriateness of behavior: "I thought Maude Lynn Dresser's snippy remark about Natalie's hat was most unbecoming, didn't you?"

The verb *become* has borne several meanings over its life. In Old English it meant "come to," which led to the broader sense of the verb today "come to be," as to become a doctor. The sense of "coming to" also led to the sense of "to receive," also found in Modern German *bekommen*. Later, in the Middle English period, it came to mean "happen to, befall." The sense of "to fit or suit" apparently has been expressed as "come to" for a long time in Indo-European languages since idët tebe, literally "it comes to you," means "it suits you" in Russian, too.

# Beleaguer ❧ *Verb, transitive*

**Pronunciation:** buh-**lee**-gur

**Beleaguer** is only slightly more beautiful than *besiege*. Today it means simply to overburden with troubles. To beleaguer is to mentally beset from all sides persistently, as to beleaguer with work or worries.

Much of the pleasure we derive from this word comes from the two rippling consonants, L and R, called 'liquids' by linguists because of their watery tone. Expect to encounter the past participle most frequently, as to be beleaguered by demands on our lives. Someone who beleaguers others is a beleaguerer, whose actions amount to beleaguerment.

We no longer waste this word's charm on military sieges but save it for the more intimate sieges of worries and concerns that plague our daily lives: "When beleaguered by the cares of office, Franklin enjoys retiring to the inner sanctum of his study to brood over the latest Grisham novel." Beleaguerment must be persistent: "Constantly beleaguered by reporters bellowing trivial questions, Lucille was beginning to regret the fame she had worked so hard to achieve."

English borrowed this one from a related Germanic language, the Dutch word *belegeren*, made up of be- "around" + leger "camp" + a verbal ending. The Proto-Indo-European root ambi "around, both (sides)," as in *ambidextrous* and *amphibian*, was reduced in Germanic languages like Dutch, English, and German to *be-*. The root of *leger* goes back to the same source as English *lair*, the root of which is *lay*. In German it emerged as *Lager*, the word for "camp," as in that ugliest of words, Konzentrationslager "concentration camp." But *Lager* also means "layer, deposit," so the beer that is produced by storing it for six months to allow a deposit of sedimentation to form is also called "lager beer."

# Brood ✨ *Verb, intransitive*

**Pronunciation:** brood

The verb **brood** originally meant to sit long and protectively on eggs, as brood hens are wont to do. This sense slipped easily into such figurative usages as clouds brooding over the horizon. Since noticeable clouds are most often dark stormy clouds, the next shift led to the sense of thinking long and darkly, usually alone.

Why is such a glum word beautiful? Well, the *u*-sound in English is long, which means we hold it longer in pronouncing it than most vowels: [bruuuuud] as compared to the much shorter word *brute* [brut]. Since brooding over eggs or problems is a long process, the long vowel in this word fits its meaning perfectly. U is also a rather dark vowel produced way in the back of the mouth, like O and A, which fits a brooding mood. A person who broods a lot is broody because of his or her broodiness.

The real beauty of this word emerges when we use it to refer to a retreat to be alone with our thoughts: "Rhoda is down by the lake brooding over a kink in the plot of her latest mystery novel." *Brood*'s very slightly pejorative sense does not spoil the beauty of its sound or meaning: "It makes no sense to brood over this; brooding won't solve the problem."

According to the lovely old Oxford English Dictionary, this word comes from an old Germanic word *bruot* "heat, warmth, hatching." We find the remnants of the original root, which was associated with heat and warmth, throughout English as well as in the vocabularies of other related languages. English *brew*, *broth*, *bread*, and German Brot "bread" and braten "bake" come from the same source as *brood*. German *braten* originated in a verb that Old French borrowed as braon "meat suitable for roasting." Middle English borrowed this word back later as *brawn*.

# Bucolic ✽ *Adjective*

**Pronunciation:** byoo-**kah**-lik, byoo-**kaw**-lik

**Bucolic** means rural, rustic, and pastoral with an additional hint of pleasure and happiness that you won't sense in these other words. Things bucolic are pleasantly rural, happily rustic, beautifully pastoral.

This word is a loner. Very marginally we find its extension, *bucolical*, which makes an adverb *bucolically* possible, but we won't find these words in anything written recently. They are no longer in circulation perhaps because they do not maintain quite the acoustic allure of *bucolic* itself.

In using this word, we never have to otherwise mention that we are speaking of happy moments in a lovely country setting: "Gwendolyn enjoyed bucolic picnics by the edge of the river on a natural carpet of wild grasses buttoned in place by yellow dandelions." That entire group of meanings is built into *bucolic*: "They bought an old farm house in a bucolic setting that invited them outside year round."

This English word was borrowed from Latin bucolicus "pastoral," copied from a Greek compound *boukolikos*. The Greek adjective was built on the noun boukolos "a cowherd," made up of bous "cow" + -kolos "herdsman." Greek *bous* comes from a Proto-Indo-European word gwou- "cow," with a shift from [gw] to [b] at the beginning of the word common in Greek. Other languages preserved the [g], as we see in Hindi *gay* "cow." The [g] became [k] in Germanic languages giving us German *Kuh*, Dutch *koe*, and English *cow*. In the Slavic languages, we find Serbian *krava* and Polish *krowa* from a root that Russian extended into *korova*.

# Bungalow ❧ *Noun*

**Pronunciation: bung-**guh-lo

A **bungalow** is a snug, cozy, one-story cottage. A bungalow may also be a small, individual hotel or motel room set aside from the main building.

This cozy little word with the cozy meaning was once upon a time written without the final W, so you may run into it spelled that way in books printed before the middle of the nineteenth century. The fact that *bungalow* has a final W but *buffalo* does not is just one of those vagaries of English spelling that make it so interesting. (Who said, "Frustrating?")

To my ear, *bungalow* connotes a warmth and comfort that *cottage* does not: "Marian Kine told Bill Arami that she didn't need a castle, just a bungalow filled with a family who enjoys sharing the housework." This word also reflects a breath of romance not found in any of its near synonyms: "Brett's anticipation of weekends with Jessica in her bungalow by the sea was beginning to crowd out all other thoughts from his mind."

This word was drawn from the Hindi word *bangle* which means "bungalow" but also, as an adjective, "Bengalese, Bengali, belonging to a Bengali." Bungalows were originally small cottages in India associated with Bengali people and the word for them is a variant of the initial element in the name of the Bengali nation, Bangladesh. As you see, not all beautiful English words were borrowed from French.

# Chinoiserie ❧ *Noun, mass*

**Pronunciation:** shin-wahz-**ree**

**Chinoiserie** means "things Chinese." Anything reflecting the Chinese culture, such as Chinese artifacts, designs, artistic styles, even behavior, is chinoiserie.

If you choose to use this word keep in mind that its original French spelling and pronunciation give it away as rather artificial and affected. Unfortunately, English offers no unaffected alternative, so just be careful of the pronunciation.

*Chinoiserie* may refer to things from China or things done in a Chinese style: "After her cruise up the Yangtze River, Gilda Lilly redecorated her apartment from top to bottom in the chinoiserie she brought back from the trip." This word may be pluralized since it can refer to individual objects: "Haifa likes to serve her Chinese dinners on a hodgepodge of the porcelain chinoiseries she collected on her trips to the Far East."

This good word, as already mentioned, is French, the noun from the adjective chinois "Chinese" itself from Chine "China." *Chine* (pronounced [sheen]) was borrowed from the Persian and Sanskrit word cinah "Chinese people." These languages picked up the word from Chinese *Ch'in* (originally *Qin*), the name of the Chinese dynasty (221–206 BC) that established the first centralized imperial government in China. Much of the Great Wall of China was built during the rule of this dynasty by the first Emperor of China, Qin Shi Huang. So, while this word is immediately of French origin, it has the history of several other languages stowed in it.

# Chatoyant ❧ *Adjective*

**Pronunciation:** shœ-**toy**-unt

Things are **chatoyant** when they are shiny and iridescent, when they have a color that changes when viewed from different angles. The *Oxford English Dictionary* calls it a "floating luster" that moves about when viewed from different angles. Certain gems, such as the moonstone, tiger-eye, and opal are chatoyant.

This resplendent Anglicized French word refers to a floating iridescent luster visible on some types of cloth, such as moiré, taffeta, satin, and especially silks like pongee and shantung. The quality of such things is chatoyance and it is possible for an object to change colors chatoyantly when viewed from different positions.

Chatoyant objects have a moveable opalescence: "In the candlelight Felicia's eyes were a chatoyant play of grays and greens with sparks of gold." It is a quality we find in surprising places: "The setting sun had spread a chatoyant array of fiery colors and shadows over the vaguely undulating surface of the lake."

French has a verb chatoyer "to shimmer, glisten," whose present participle is chatoyant "shimmering, glistening." It was created from the noun chat "cat," a word referring to a friendly beast with chatoyant eyes. English borrowed this participle for its lovely adjective. The origin of *chat* is the same as that of English *cat*, Vulgar (street) Latin *cattus*, but no one knows where this word came from or why it seems to have replaced not only Classical Latin felix "cat" (origin of English *feline*) but Greek *ailouros* too, the root of *ailurophile*.

# 𝒞omely ✂ *Adjective*

## Pronunciations: kum-li

**Comely** things are pretty, attractive, fair, of moderate beauty. This word can also serve to indicate that which is seemly, polite, or becoming.

Like all adjectives with the suffix *-ly*, such as *friendly*, *motherly*, and *sisterly*, *comely* is its own adverb. No language likes to repeat itself, so *comelily* is out of the question on grammatical as well as aesthetic grounds. Because of the confusion with the adjective, however, the adverb has been rarely used since the seventeenth century: "He spoke quite comely of his sister." The noun from this adjective is a rather comely word itself: *comeliness*.

If you wish to express the sentiment of prettiness, why not use a pretty word? *Comely* is a verbal flower that will decorate any conversation: "I find Maggie a remarkably comely woman in feature and mind, don't you?" It also has the advantage of referring to actions as well as things: "I didn't think it very comely of Harold to shake hands with the men and kiss the women in the reception line."

*Comely* is a word of absolute English origin. It can be traced back to Old English cymlic "lovely, delicate" from cyme "beautiful," and is not directly related to the verb *come*. It is related, however, to the second meaning of *become*, as in a hat that becomes you or behavior unbecoming an officer. The suffix *-ly* was whittled down by time from Old English lic which went on to become *like*. It is interesting that lic was a word that became a suffix in words like *manly* and *fatherly*. Now, it would seem that the modern version of the same word is repeating the process in words such as *man-like* and *father-like*.

# ℭonflate ∾ *Verb, transitive*

**Pronunciation:** kun-**flayt**

To **conflate** is to collapse and combine into one, to blend two or more things into one.

This bonny word is the only one we know that precisely expresses the concept of reducing and combining several things to one. Neither *collapse* nor *combine* is this specific, which means that this word is an important term for any vocabulary. The noun is *conflation*. No related adjective seems to have survived, though conflatable "capable of being conflated" is certainly a potentiality.

*Conflation* is not simply the mixing of two things together (as dictionaries often claim), but the blending and reduction of them to one: "Our marriage counselor told us that all our problems reside in the difficulty of conflating the schedules of two lives into one." This word is often used in reference to written material: "By conflating her roommate's blog and diary, and plagiarizing the result, Rhoda Book created a prize-winning novel."

This beautiful word goes back to Latin conflare "to blow together, melt, fuse (metals)" from con- "with, together" + flare "blow." The basic verb, *flare*, shares a source with English *blow* and *bladder*. Blowing a fire results in a blaze, another related word, though this one blew in from Dutch blasen "to blow up." The Latin stem is also found in *inflate*, *flatulent*, and via French, *soufflé*. Soufflé "puffed up" is past participle of souffler "to puff up," a word inherited from Latin *sufflare*, based on sub- "(from) below" plus the same *flare* that went into the making of *conflate*

# Cynosure ✎ *Noun*

**Pronunciation: sin**-uh-shUr, **sai**-nuh-shUr

The **Cynosure** (capitalized) is the constellation Ursa Minor or the North Star that lies within it. Since the North Star has been a guidepost for mariners for ages, we may now use this word uncapitalized to refer to anything that leads or provides guidance. The focal point or center of attention may also be called a cynosure.

This word is strikingly beautiful, especially when pronounced [**si**-nuh-shUr] In *L'Allegro* (1645) Milton wrote, "Where perhaps some Beauty lies, The Cynosure of neighbouring eyes." There is an adjective, *cynosural*, not to mention an adverb, *cynosurally*, either of which you might enjoy weaving into conversations.

*Cynosure* is usually associated with something or someone lustrously attractive: "The silver evening gown in which Lila lilted luxuriantly down the stairs made her the immediate cynosure of the party." But we can expand the meaning as well, since the word originally referred to a constellation that provided guidance to mariners: "Seamus's house is of such bizarrely eccentric design that it serves as the cynosure for directions to all the other homes in his neighborhood."

The roots of this elegant word reveal an impressive historical span from the profane to the celestial. It started out long ago as a Greek word of considerably less beauty: kynosoura "dog-tail," a compound noun comprising kuon, kynos "dog" + oura "tail." The root, *kwon-, from which kuon derives, also gave rise to English *hound* and Latin canis "dog." Latin *canis*, in turn, is the source of English *canine* and the *Canary* in *Canary Islands*. The name of these islands was originally Latin Canariae Insulae "Islands of the Dogs"; English simply adapted the spelling in borrowing it.

# Dalliance ✺ *Noun*

**Pronunciation: dæ**-li-juns

A **dalliance** may be a simple bit of dawdling, strolling casually or a bit of dallying in the sense of a frivolous affair, a flitting romance, or even an extended flirtation.

*Affair* itself is not an ugly word but *dalliance* adds a slightly mysterious diaphanous quality to the idea. *Dalliance* contains a group of sonorous sounds, L, N, and breezy S—a recipe for lexical pulchritude. *Dalliance* also breathes an intimation of *alliance* well aligned with its meaning. It is the noun for the verb *dally*, which means "to fiddle around" with all its implications.

My own feeling is that dalliances should only be undertaken in romantic settings: "After a summer-long dalliance with a charming young man in Tuscany, Daphne returned to the humdrumming of her job at the Pentagon." However, this word does carry a trace of humor not to be ignored: "Phil Ander's office dalliances have led him down the garden path many times but never to the altar."

This bewitchingly fluid word is the noun from the verb *dally*, which means to lag behind, move slowly without focus. It originally meant "to chat idly," a meaning that came with it when it was borrowed from Old French *dalier*. Old French borrowed this word from a Germanic language, perhaps Dutch, where *taal* means "language, speech." English added a suffix -k to the ancestor of *taal*, making it *talk* but, since the K doesn't show up in the French, Dutch or Low German is the more likely source of French *dalier*. English also made a rhyming compound out of this verb: *dilly-dally*, meaning only to lag behind or move even more nonchalantly than *dallying*.

# Demesne ✤ *Noun*

## Pronunciation: duh-**mayn**

A **demesne** is an estate, the land and property owned by someone, possibly a district, region, territory, or realm belonging to an overlord or nobleman. It is more or less the same as a domain or dominion. In legalese this word implies the full ownership and right use of a piece of land.

This word is a more beautiful surrogate for *domain* in *domain*'s general though not in its abstract sense, as the domain of someone's knowledge. Unlike *domain, demesne* is rather overspelled: aside from the silent E at the end of it, beware the internal silent S.

If a person's home is his or her castle, the yard it sits upon is his or her demesne: "I love my little demesne in the country; if only I didn't have to mow it." Demesnes are everywhere; you probably have several in your neighborhood: "The principal may make the rules, but the school is the demesne of the head custodian, without whom nothing would work."

This word is an excellent example of why spelling is so important. *Demesne* is a re-Frenchification of Middle English *demeine*, a respelling by influential Francophiles in the seventeenth century. The new spelling was influenced by mesne "lord of a manor or estate," a word related to *manse* and maison "house." Under the influence of *dominion*, Old French *demeine* became Modern French *domaine* which English, in its usual borrowing frenzy, also collected. Both spellings issued over time from Latin dominicus "belonging to a lord," the adjective from dominus "lord." *Dominus* comes from the same root as *dome, domestic*, and *dominate*, and Russian and Polish dom "house."

# Ðemure ✒ *Adjective*

**Pronunciation:** di-**myur**

You are **demure** if you are reserved to the point of shyness, if you are a person understated and underspoken. This word is also used tongue-in-cheek to refer to people who coyly pretend to be reserved, who are affectedly shy or modest.

The trick to this word lies in the avoidance of any confusion with the very similar verb, *demur* [duh-**mur**], which means either to show reluctance, be hesitant or, in legal proceedings, to object that certain facts do not bear on an argument. You may say, "Theo rightfully demurred from giving the caller the number of his checking account." *Demure* (with long U and silent E) is an adjective with a distinctively different pronunciation and meaning. The usual noun associated with it is *demureness* but I rather like an older one, *demurity*.

Did you ask if I could work both these confusing words into one sentence? Listen to this: "Charlotte Russe demurred from the offer of a second dessert, waiting until asked a second time, at which point she demurely accepted." This word may suggest pretended modesty: "When the distraught man asked if she had any knowledge of car engines, the retired mechanic replied, 'A smattering,' with a demure smile."

The verb *demur* came into English from French demeurer "to delay," from Latin demorari "to delay," built upon de "from, un-" + mora "a delay." *Demure* seems to originate with Old French meur "discreet," a reduction of Latin maturus "mature," though the prefix de- here is a bit puzzling. The *mat-* in Latin maturus is the same as that in *matinee* from French matin "morning," related to Spanish *mañana*, Portuguese *amanhã*, and Romanian *mâine*, all meaning "tomorrow." All three of these words come from Latin mane [**mah**-nay] "in the morning."

# Denouement ❧ *Noun*

## Pronunciation: de-nu-**mawN**

The **denouement** of a drama or narrative work is the clarification and unraveling of all mystery following the climax of a story. It can also be the climax itself if the climax includes the resolution of a complex set of mysterious events that makes everything clear to everyone.

This word has all the properties of a French word. We can even accent the first E, if we wish, *dénouement*, but this word remains out in the English world all alone. It has been in the language only since the latter half of the eighteenth century and hence has no derivational relatives. Just be sure to include the E at the end of the row of three vowels (oue) in the middle of this word, a rather unusual phenomenon in English.

A denouement is not simply a climax but one that resolves all outstanding questions: "The denouement of their long and convoluted divorce was a decision to make up and continue living together." Each episode of the TV series *Murder, She Wrote* concludes with a denouement in which the heroine, J. B. Fletcher, explains how she followed all the clues to the resolution of the mystery, thus clearing up any residual questions.

French dénouement "untying, releasing" comes from the verb dénouer "to untie," made up of dé- "from, un-" plus nouer "to tie." The French word for "tie" comes from the noun nœud "knot," a historical reduction of Latin nodus "knot," which, by the way, English *node* is based on. We changed the same word quite a bit more to create the word *noose*. The same Proto-Indo-European stem came directly to English via its Germanic ancestors as *net* and *nettle*. The fibers of nettles long ago went into the making of the rope and cord that go into the making of nets.

# Desuetude ❧ *Noun, mass*

## Pronunciation: de-swuh-tyood

**Desuetude** is a comelier way of saying "disuse, inactivity."

This noun was made from an archaic adjective *desuete*, which itself fell into desuetude in the early eighteenth century. *Desuetude* has probably survived on the strength of its beauty alone. It is now a true lexical orphan, without any surviving lexical kin.

This is not a word you would use chatting with the boys of the motorcycle club in the sports bar, but it is very much at home in more elegant settings: "The rituals of courtship seem to be tumbling into complete desuetude in the modern world." This doesn't mean that it can't carry its own weight in the ordinary world: "Watching political campaigns today, you would think that common civility had fallen into complete desuetude."

This word is simply French *désuétude* without its diacritical decorations (which you may keep if you enjoy them) and with an English accent. It is the remains of Latin *desuetudo*, a noun created from *desuetus*, the past participle of *desuescere* "to put out of use." *Desuescere*, in its turn, is composed of de- "reverse, undo" + suescere "to become accustomed to." The root of *suescere* is *sui* "oneself," as in sui generis "unique, in a class all its own." We also see this reflexive pronoun in *suicide* "self-murder." It shares a source with *swami*, which English borrowed from Sanskrit svami "master of oneself." Russian svoi "oneself" goes back to the same root.

# Desultory ❧ *Adjective*

**Pronunciation: de**-zul-tor-ee

**Desultory** implies a slow meandering, floating aimlessly without course or direction and, by extension, to anything random, haphazard, or simply disorganized.

This adjective drifted off on its own and left its mother far behind some years ago. It was originally the offspring of desultor "a leaping equestrian," but now bears no semantic relationship to that word. It bears all the accoutrements of English adjectives, including an adverb *desultorily* and a noun *desultoriness*.

As I wrote this, I was watching desultory leaves falling from the sugar maple in my back yard. You might have thought at the time that they were choosing a spot to land, given the elaborately composed carpet of yellow they were spreading across the lawn. All that is over now and I have just returned with my family from the desultory holiday weekend to focus again on work.

Latin desultor "leaper" referred to a Roman circus performer who rode several horses at one time, leaping from one to the other. This word was derived from *desultus*, the past participle of desilire "to leap from," based on de- "from, un-" + salire "to jump." The root *salire* is indirectly responsible for salacious "lustful, wanton," taken from Latin salax "fond of leaping." (I'll let you connect the semantic dots.) Something that is salient leaps out at you and when you sally forth, you leap out yourself. *Salire* is responsible for both these words. We are not sure of this, but *salmon* may have come from a word meaning "leaping fish," long since lost. This would certainly explain the *sal-* in this word.

# Diaphanous ❧ *Adjective*

**Pronunciation:** dai-æ-fuh-nus

Things **diaphanous** are soft, thin, filmy and translucent, if not utterly transparent. They are fragile, flimsy, likely to dissipate under the slightest stress.

Remember that this most beautiful word comes from Greek, so the [f] sound is spelled PH, an alluring graphic complication of the word. The adverb is *diaphanously*. The noun, *diaphanousness*, sounds a bit ponderous to me, so I prefer the lighter sound of *diaphaneity* [dai-æf-uh-**nee**-uh-tee].

Gowns and veils are most likely to be diaphanous; however, there might be days when we would enjoy strolling in a diaphanous fog or drizzle. The meaning "flimsiness" lends itself to many other situations: "Jonathan's lie was so diaphanous, a blind man could see through it." Fragility is another inclination that has crept into this word: "Frank's idea was so diaphanous, it evaporated before anyone could comment on it." This is one of those words you want to share purely for its beauty.

*Diaphanous* was reworked from Greek diaphanes "transparent," based on dia- "through" + phainein "to show." Phainein contains the same root as *photo-*, found in many words. We also see it in Greek phantasia "appearance, imagination," from phantos "visible." Latin borrowed this Greek word and passed it down to French as *fantasie*, which English converted to *fantasy*. The original Proto-Indo-European root, *bhaa- "shine, flow," percolated directly through the Germanic languages to end up in such English words as *buoy*, *beckon*, *beacon*, and *berry*; the latter apparently started out its life meaning "shiny fruit."

# Dissemble ✒ *Verb*

## Pronunciation: dis-**sem**-bul

**Dissembling** is not taking things apart; it is pretending, giving a false or misleading semblance of something. It means to mislead, deceive, or misguide.

This lovely word is a more mellifluous substitute for *deceive* or *mislead*. It is completely unrelated to *disassemble* and hence should not be confused with this word in spelling or pronunciation. A dissembler dissembles until caught in his or her dissemblance. (Well, some continue their dissemblance even after having been caught at it.)

Dissemblance can be simple fakery: "The fact that Cranston dissembled most of his credentials became painfully apparent the first day he took up the duties of his new job." Anything you intentionally disguise is dissembled: "I cannot dissemble my love of your chocolate torte, Myra. Could I have just one more slice?"

This genteel old word was captured from Old French dessembler "to be different," a word made up of dis- "not" + sembler "to appear, seem." It comes from the same ultimate source as English *resemble*, *similar*, and *simulate*, the Proto-Indo-European root sem- "one, as one." These three words were borrowed from French, but the same root became *same* in English, homos "same" in Greek," sam "together" in Sanskrit, and sam "self" in Russian. The Russian word turns up in two English borrowings: *samovar*, literally "self-boiler," and *samizdat* "self-publishing."

# Dulcet ❧ *Adjective*

## Pronunciation: dul-set

*Dulcet* means sweet-sounding, soft and musical.

If **dulcet** reminds you of the sounds of a dulcimer, that isn't coincidental: the two words share he same origin. Besides the suggestion of a dulcimer, the connotation of dullness in the sense of softness far removed from glare or harshness, also adds to this word's beauty. You may use the adverb *dulcetly* and the noun *dulcetness* if you wish, but the commonplace suffixes attached to these derivations rob the underlying word of much of its allure.

The phonetic and semantic attractiveness of this word more than justifies its frequency in romantic poetry and literature: "The dulcet solo of a lark wafted through her garden, dissolving everything into a vivid moment she would never forget." The challenge is to shepherd this word carefully through our conversations and not overplay it: "The dulcet tones of Mary Louise's voice calmed the excited child quickly and he fell asleep in only a few minutes."

English borrowed this word from Old French before the L's in that language changed into Us, converting it to doucet "meek, mild." The [l] sound met the same fate in *doux* (feminine *douce*) "sweet." French inherited the word from Latin dulcis "sweet," to which it added the suffix *-et*. Many etymologists think that Greek glukus "sweet," which English borrowed for *glucose*, came from the same root, though they are taxed to explain the shift of [d] to [g] and I can offer no explanation.

# Ebullience ⚬ *Adjective*

**Pronunciation:** i-**bUl**-yunts

**Ebullience** began its life referring to boiling or bubbling and in some contexts it can still be used in this sense. Today, though, it is more often used to refer to metaphorical bubbling, a bubbling over of the spirits, exuberance, cheerful enthusiasm.

This pearl of lexical fancy was derived from the adjective *ebullient*, itself from the out-dated verb ebulliate "to boil," no longer used in polite company. Like all adjectives ending on NT, *ebullient* creates a noun by simply adding the suffix -*s*, though we must remember to spell it *ebullience*.

Since we often attribute animacy to inanimate objects, we can succumb to the temptation to use this comely term in the description of excited liquids: "Lionel and Penny loved their intimate picnics by the ebullient spring that tittered through the field behind their house." However, this word most commonly appears in descriptions of us mortals: "Maria's ebullience for her job often caused infectious ripples across staff meetings."

*Ebullience* came to us from Latin *ebullien(t)s*, the present participle of ebullire "to bubble up." It comprises a reduction of the prefix ex- "up, from, out of" + bullire "to bubble, boil." The same root turns up in Germanic languages reduplicated from an early form *bul-bul-*, which went on to become Swedish *bubbla*, Danish *boble*, and Dutch *bobble*. In English it developed in two directions, becoming *bubble* and *burble*. The sound of all these words was strongly influenced by the bubbling sound of turbulent or boiling water.

# Efflorescence ∽ *Noun, mass*

**Pronunciation:** ef-luh-**re**-sents

In its essence, **efflorescence** is simply flowering, blossoming, certainly a decorative thought. It has been extended, though, to any slow unfurling or development, especially that reaching a peak or the fulfillment of a potential. To chemists, it refers to chemical bloom, deposits of salts left by the evaporation of fluids containing minerals, or the process of making such deposits.

Words with the French suffix *-escence*, like *evanescence*, *effervescence*, and *quiescence*, are lexical flowers themselves; all have a beautiful sound, most corresponding with visually beautiful meanings. This word is the noun based on the adjective efflorescent "blooming," associated with the verb, (to) *effloresce*.

Efflorescence originally referred simply to the blossoming of flowers: "The efflorescence of the azaleas and dogwood coincides every spring during the Azalea Festival in Wilmington." It can also be used in as many figurative senses as English's own *blossoming*: "Graham's efflorescence into a sterling violinist by the age of twelve surprised everyone who knew that he could not tie his shoes."

This word comes from a verb, *effloresce*, borrowed from Latin efflorescere "to bloom forth," made up of ex "from, out of" + *florescere*, an extension of florer "to blossom." *Florer* was derived from flos, flor- "flower," found in many Latin borrowings such as *floral*, *florist*, the name *Flora*, and the Italian city of Florence. The F at the beginning of these Latin words came from an original [bh] sound ([b] with a puff of air) which went on to become regular [b] in English. That is why the corresponding words in English generally begin with a B, as is the case with *bloom* and *blossom*.

# Elision ❧ *Noun*

**Pronunciation:** i-**li**-zhun

**Elision** is the omission of sounds or syllables in a word, such as the pronunciation of *police* as "p'lice" or *pollution* as "p'lution." It is often represented by an apostrophe, as in the case of contractions like *can't, I'll,* and *I'd've*.

This word is the process noun from the verb elide [uh-**laid**]. The adjective is *elisional*. It is used widely by linguists in reference to unaccented vowels that drop out of words in the process of linguistic change. Don't confuse *elision* with *ellipsis*, the omission of words that are unnecessary or irrelevant from a sentence, usually indicated by a triplet of periods (…). This group of dots itself is also called an ellipsis.

The elision of initial syllables is very noticeable in the Southern dialects where *opossum* becomes *'possum, potato* becomes *'tater,* and *alligator* is simply *'gator*. But internal elision of unaccented vowels is rampant in all dialects of English, where we hear *s'pose* for *suppose, prob'ly* (even *prol'ly*) for *probably,* and many others. The process doesn't leave a pretty result but the word for it is absolutely captivating.

This word is derived from the verb *elide*, which comes via French from Latin elidere "to omit, strike out," based on e(x) "from, out of" + laedere "to strike, damage." We don't know where this root came from and it does not seem to have developed in other Indo-European languages. We do find it in at least two more English words borrowed from Latin. Allision "crashing into" comes from ad "(up) to" + *laedere* while collision "crashing together" comes from com- "together (with)" + *laedere*. So, if we wish to be precise, a moving object crashing into an immoveable object results in an allision, while a collision comes from two moving objects striking each other.

# Elixir ❧ *Noun*

**Pronunciation:** uh-**lik**-sur

**Elixirs** were originally substances purportedly capable of converting base metals to gold. From here it was but a short skip to the sense of a preparation that gives everlasting life by curing all ills and maladies, in short, a liquid panacea.

Historically, the meaning of this word has skidded about quite a bit. It has been used to refer to quack medicines like snake oil and, in pharmacology, it is still used to refer to an admixture to a medicine that makes it taste better. Today it seems to have settled in on the sense of a draft that solves all problems and resolves all issues.

An elixir is not a medicine for a specific malady but rather a cure-all, a magic potion for a complex mess: "There is no magical elixir that will repair all the damage your philandering has done to our relationship, Phil." The elixir of life is what flows in the Fountain of Youth: "I would like to believe, my dear, that champagne is the elixir of life that can prolong my existence indefinitely."

This lovely word went 'round and 'round before arriving in English. English borrowed the word from Late (Medieval) Latin *elixir*. It had somehow slipped into Latin from Arabic al-'iksir, *al* "the" + *'iksir* "elixir" (in the original sense). How did this word come to be in Arabic? It probably was borrowed from Greek *xerion* "desiccative powder." *Xerion* was a powder used to dry wounds, derived from *xeros* "dry." *Xeros* was also the origin of the English *Xerox*, the brand name of the first copier using a dry rather than wet ink-based system.

# Eloquence ✎ *Noun, mass*

**Pronunciation: el**-uh-kwents

**Eloquence** is not necessarily beautiful speech but it is moving spoken or written language, language that is persuasive by virtue of its cleverness and beauty.

This word is itself eloquent in both sound and meaning, producing a tight fit between the two. It is the noun derived from the adjective *eloquent*, which comes with an adverb *eloquently*. Although another gift from France, this word has been thoroughly adapted to English so that all its sounds are now genuinely English.

Eloquence is usually associated with speech: "Arthur detected a decline in the eloquence of the conversations with his wife after the children came along." Do not think for a moment, though, that eloquence is limited to speech: "The Statue of Liberty speaks with great eloquence of the millions of immigrants who came and created the USA and its language."

*Eloquence* is the French remodeling of Latin *elocutio(n)*, the noun from elocutus "spoken out," past participle of *eloqui* "to speak out." Again we see English borrowing the same word at different points in its career as two different words: *elocution* and *eloquence. Eloqui* is composed of e(x) "from, out (of)" + *loqui* "to speak." *Loqui* comes from the Proto-Indo-European word tolkw- "to speak," which ended up as English *talk* and Russian tolkovat' "to interpret." It is possible that the O and L underwent metathesis (switched places) in early Latin, resulting in a root *tlokw-*. If this occurred, the initial T would have disappeared since Latin did not permit TL at the beginning of a word. The result would be a word pronounced [lokwi] and spelled *loqui*.

# Embrocation ✎ *Noun*

**Pronunciation:** em-bruh-**kay**-shun

**Embrocation** is the action of rubbing with a lotion, ointment, or liniment. It can also indicate the soothing or healing reaction to such rubbing with a lotion or, finally, the liquid itself used in embrocation, as an embrocation of perfumed ointment.

*Embrocation* is the noun derived from the verb embrocate "to rub with an oil or lotion," a normal if rare Latinate verb. *Embrocator*, the person who embrocates someone, and *embrocational*, the adjective, are acceptable derivations even though my spell-checker does not seem to be acquainted with them.

What mother hasn't said at some time: "Don't go out on the beach without a liberal embrocation of sunscreen!" Well, if you haven't heard your mother say something like that, what a treat you have missed! This word is much lovelier than *slather* or *fomentation*, the first meaning of which is also "to apply liquids or lotions to the body." Remember that an embrocation is also the liquid itself used in the process of embrocation: "Oh, how I wish I had a magic embrocation for the wrinkles in my face and those in my plans."

This soothing word comes from the noun of the Medieval Latin verb embrocare "to rub with ointment" from Late Latin embrocha "lotion." The Latin word was borrowed from Greek embrokhe "lotion," the noun of embrekhein "to rub with lotion" made up of en- "in" + brekhein "to rain, to moisten." The original root apparently began with an M, for we find related words beginning with M in a few other Indo-European languages, such as Russian morosit' "to drizzle."

# Emollient ❧ *Adjective, Noun*

## Pronunciation: i-**mahl**-yunt

As an adjective, **emollient** means "softening, soothing" as an embrocation with an emollient effect on the skin. The sense of soothing may be metaphorical as an emollient conversation with someone who has lost their temper. As a noun, *emollient* refers to an agent with an emollient effect, as a skin or leather emollient.

Almost all adjectives ending on -*ent* may be used as adjectives and nouns, as may this word. It is the present participial suffix in French, corresponding to -*ing* in English. Like all such adjectives, the noun referring to the quality suggested by the adjective is spelled by simply adding the *s*-sound to the adjective but spelling it, as do the French, -*ence*. So, *emollience* would mean "softening" or simply "softness," though it is rarely used.

Emolument "pay, compensation" is actually more musical than *emollient* but its meaning is less felicitous, so I prefer *emollient*: "Jerry could always expect an emollient word from his wife when he returned home each day from a pounding at the office." Don't forget that this word works as well as a noun: "Lucille's homemade herbal emollients left her skin very soft to the touch but with a slight tinge of greenness."

This lovely word began as Latin mollis "soft," which was verbalized as emollire "to soften." The present participle of this verb was emollien(t)s "softening," which English took over, dropping the final S but keeping the T. The root word, *mollis*, is a member of an Indo-European family that includes Russian molodoy "young" and English *melt* and *mild*. The oddity of this family might seem to be the word *mollusk*, a family of hard-shelled animals that include snails and shellfish. The softness hidden in the meaning of this word refers, of course, to the inner animals themselves, and not their shells.

# Ephemeral ∽ *Adjective*

**Pronunciation:** i-**fe**-muh-rul

Originally, **ephemeral** meant "lasting one day only." That meaning expanded over the years until it now refers to anything very short-lived, fleeting, lasting extremely briefly.

This lovely word still pops up occasionally in its original sense. For example, insects that live for only a day are ephemeral insects, diseases that last but a day are ephemeral diseases, and we sometimes suffer an ephemeral fever. The scientific name for a bad hair day is 'the ephemeral ague.' *Ephemerality* is the noun and *ephemerally*, the adverb form of this adjective.

This word is used most widely in reference to events of very short duration: "An ephemeral smile jostled her lips at his joke, but her attention quickly returned to the filet." This word stands out among others for its phonetic beauty and its reference to pleasant things that do not last long enough: "Her ephemeral romance with the president left Bambi with no higher position to conquer."

This word was borrowed from Greek ephemeros "lasting a day, daily" from epi- "on" + hemera "day." The pronunciation really should be a far less lovely [ep-**he**-muh-rul], but the PH came to be pronounced F in Greek, giving us the lovelier word we have today. The Greek preposition epi "on" shares its origins with Latin ob "against" and Russian o(b) "around, against." Neither this root nor that of *hemera* seem to have survived among the Germanic languages.

# Epiphany ❧ *Noun*

**Pronunciation:** i-**pif**-uh-nee

Capitalized (**Epiphany**), this word refers to the Christian celebration on January 6 of the visit of the three Magi to the newly
born Jesus Christ. Without capitalization, it can refer to the
sudden appearance of any divine being or simply a profound
insight brought on suddenly by some experience, usually with
spiritual or at least metaphysical overtones.

Despite this word's having passed through Latin on its way to
English, it has produced only two relatives, the adjective *epipha-
nic* [e-pi-**fæn**-ik] and an adverb, *epiphanically*, but that is the end
of the derivational line of *epiphany*.

Epiphanies are sudden, brought on by some event that has a profound effect: "Talking with you the other night, Madeleine, I had
an epiphany when I suddenly realized how important children, a
family, and a home are to me." An epiphany is more than a bright
idea, though; it must make a profound difference in the way we
behave: "After twenty years planning for the future, Dennis one
day had an epiphany and realized that he should live his life as if
every day were his last."

Like so many English words, this lovely creature comes to us
from Latin *epiphania* via French. The Romans picked it up from
Greek epiphaneia "manifestation," from epiphainein "to mani-
fest, display," made up of epi "on, over" + phainein "to show."
The same root also went into the making of Greek theophaneia
"revelation by a god," derived from theos "god" + phainein "to
show, reveal." Latin borrowed this word and passed it on to Old
French, where it was reduced to *tiphanie*. At this point English
borrowed it, respelled the [f] sound, and used it to name *tiffany*,
the thin gauzy muslin fabric—and the family responsible for the
expensive jewelry and colorful lamps bearing its name.

# Erstwhile ❧ *Adjective, Adverb*

## Pronunciation: urst-hwail

**Erstwhile** works fine as an adjective or adverb meaning former(ly), previous(ly) or, to mention another attractive real English word, *whilom*.

This beautiful word has been orphaned by age. All its immediate relatives are long since dead or are in serious condition. It is amazing that we still occasionally read it and, in academia at least, hear it from time to distantly displaced time. Should we forget *erst*, we may use the *while* in this word alone if only we suffix it properly with *-om*, for *whilom* means the same thing: "He is the whilom editor of *The Good Speler's Guide*."

I recommend *erstwhile* because it is less formal and a bit sexier than *former*: "Mel Bourne's dalliance with that erstwhile beauty queen from Sydney—Alice Springs, I think her name is—has come a cropper, I'm afraid." This word works just as well as an adverb: "The bears that erstwhile teemed in the forest now spend their days prowling around the city garbage dump."

This beautiful word is made up of two solidly English words, one of which is easily recognizable: *erst* + *while*. *While* comes from Old English *hwil*, which goes back to an ancient root kwei- "to rest, be quiet." In addition to *while*, it produced quies "quiet" in Latin, which became *quei* in Old French and coi "quiet, speechless" in Modern French. English borrowed it as *coy*. *Erst* started out as the superlative degree of the adverb (preposition, conjunction) ere "before, earlier," as to leave ere morning breaks along the horizon (conjunction). In fact, that is it before the suffix *-ly* in *early*. The superlative, *erst*, originally meant "earliest" and, yes, it is related to German erst "first."

# Ethereal ✎ *Adjective*

**Pronunciation:** i-**thi**-ree-ul

Things **ethereal** are flimsy, wispy, airy, floating along the edge of existence. In fact, an object ethereal may be positively ghostly, not of this world at all but barely visible. In the world of chemistry, this word is used in reference to ether.

This charming word is the adjective from *ether* which, to the ancient Greeks, was the crystal clear upper air breathed by the gods of Olympus. That is where the sense of "airiness" originated. This word may be used adverbially as *ethereally*. The quality it represents is *ethereality*. While this word's sound and meaning alone are beautiful, the poetic if rather archaic spelling, *æthereal*, with the *ae*-ligature, gives it an even more angelic and…well…ethereal appearance.

Spirits are the most likely creatures to be ethereal: "Charlene? She just swept swiftly through the house without speaking to anyone like an ethereal spirit on a mission." Untouchable objects are also ethereal: "Sidney Couch putters around an ethereal garden of images and ideas in his mind and has very little contact with the real world."

*Ether* comes to English from Greek *aither*, the pure upper air breathed by the gods on Mount Olympus. This word, interestingly enough, is a noun from the verb aithein "to ignite, light, set on fire." The connection would seem to be either the ethereality of fire or the fact that fires were kept in the temples of the gods. The latter is suggested by a Latin word of the same origin, aedis "temple, building." This word is at the bottom of Latin *ædificium*, which came to English, via French as usual, as *edifice*.

# Evanescent ❧ *Adjective*

**Pronunciation:** e-vuh-**ne**-sunt

Fleeting, dissipating softly, tending to evaporate or simply disappear softly into thin air. Ethereal things tend to be evanescent, barely there at all.

*Evanescent* is the daughter of the verb *evanesce* and the mother of the noun *evanescence*. Objects in a fog tend to come in and out of view *evanescently*—the adverb. The softness in the sense of *evanescent* sustains the beauty of this word's sound and justifies its inclusion in this collection.

Because *evanescent* is so exquisite, it often emerges in tender romantic situations: "The sight of Abby's evanescent breath in the chilly air made Ford's heart race a little faster yet." However, it makes the rounds in others, as well: "You don't realize how evanescent youth really is until forget your own name."

This word is Latin evanescen(t)s "vanishing," the present participle of evanescere "to vanish," in English guise. This Latin verb comprises e(x)- "from, out of" + vanescere "to vanish," another verb that ended up in the English lexicon, a bit more disguised, as *vanish*. At the root of this verb is the adjective vanus "empty," which came from the same source as English *wane* and *vain*, each referring to its own kind of emptiness. It is also related to Latin vacare "to be empty," which underlies several English borrowings, such as *vacant*, *vacation*, not to mention *vast*.

# Evocative ✎ *Adjective*

**Pronunciation:** ee-**vah**-kuh-tiv

**Evocative** means calling to mind, eliciting memories, usually pleasant ones, bringing thoughts forward from the far corners of the psyche.

Although this fetching word is built on the verb *evoke*, its meaning is constrained narrowly to one of that verb's senses: "to call forth memories." It comes garnished with several pleasant associations. It is itself evocative of the word *eve*, the poetic alternative for *evening* and a lovely feminine name (*Eve*) remindful of the Garden of Eden. We may use it as an adverb, *evocatively*, or convert it to the noun *evocativeness*.

Here is a word that replaces several inferiors, such as *going back to, recalling, harkening back to*, among others: "Gilda Lilly loves clothing styles evocative of her youth, of growing up in Adelaide in the 1940s." Objects of any reminiscence are evocative, though: "Cy O'Nara wrote a lovely ballad evocative of the homelands of his father and mother, Ireland and Japan, respectively."

*Evocative* is a borrowing from a French adjective derived from Latin evocare "to call forth" from e(x) "from, out of" + vocare "to call." We can all think of other words borrowed from Latin containing this word's root: *vocation* (calling), *vocal*, *provoke*, *equivocal*, and *convoke* "to call together." Etymologists are convinced it produced another beautiful word: *calliope*. *Calliope* comes from Greek kalliope "beautifully voiced," reshaped from kallos "beauty" + ops "voice." Etymologists can trace Greek ops "voice" back to the same source that gave Latin its root voc-, the source of *voice*. The proof is not pretty, though, so has no business here.

# Fetching ❧ *Adjective*

**Pronunciation: fe**-ching

Things that are **fetching** fall somewhere between pretty and beautiful on the beauty scale. Because it implies attracting the eye, its meaning parallels those of *attractive* and *alluring*, but it also suggests a simplicity not sensed in the other two.

Sometimes the beauty of an object comes from the fact that it is simply far more beautiful than the thing it is made from. This word falls to the category of beauty surprisingly arises from floppy hats, freckled faces, and handmade necklaces. *Fetch* is not a particularly attractive word but its participle is, probably because the suffix *-ing* adds a tinkle to its sound. Somehow, the participle has picked up the sense of "pretty" itself, elevating it to a position in this book. You may use it as an adverb so long as you remember to add the adverb suffix: *fetchingly*

This word is usually applied to people and things they wear: "Natalie Cladd arrived at church in a fetching outfit with a white skirt, accented by a flourish of blossoms on the side, and a peach sweater." *Fetching* also applies comfortably to pretty much anything artistic that we do: "Maude Lynn Singer performed a fetching little ditty from Ireland that surprised her audience to no end."

The idea behind *fetching* resembles that behind *attractive*: so lovely as to attract (fetch) attention. *Fetch* goes back to Old English *fetian* "to fetch, bring, to marry," the ablaut e-variant of Old English fot "foot." Fetching things in the original sense of the verb was 'footing it' after that object. The adjective *fetching* itself appeared in the 1570s meaning "crafty, scheming." It was only in the 1880s that it picked up the sense of "pretty."

# Felicity ∾ *Adjective*

**Pronunciation:** fuh-li-suh-tee

This lovely lexical lady began life meaning joy and happiness, implying good fortune or a stroke of luck. **Felicity** ended up referring to beauty or gracefulness, particularly in the use of language. All three senses combine in a charmingly compatible bouquet.

This word is possessed of such mellifluous sound and pleasant meaning, that it was once a popular name for girls. Today it is at the center of attention in a family of related words, such as the adjective *felicitous* and the verb *felicitate* "to make happy." Should you ever need a shorter synonym of the adjective *felicitous*, you might try *felicious*, which has the added charm of rhyming with *delicious*. Do be mindful, though, that it hasn't been much used since the eighteenth century).

We often wish someone the felicities of a particular holiday or celebration: "Felix dropped by to deliver a bouquet of flowers and wish us every felicity for the Christmas season." However, this word has a particularly felicitous relationship with writing style: "The felicities in Rhoda Book's writing style are so numerous and exquisite as to suggest that she may have a brilliant career as a novelist."

This word came from French félicité "happiness," which evolved from Latin felicitas "happy, fortunate." Beneath this noun lies the adjective felix "lucky, auspicious," borrowed as a name in English, as in Felix Unger of Neil Simon's *The Odd Couple*, and Felix the Cat of comic book fame. The root *fel-* would seem to be related to Latin fellare "to suckle," filius "son" and filia "daughter." What better source for the sense of good fortune, grace, and beauty?

# Forbearance ∽ *Noun*

**Pronunciation:** for-**ber**-unts

**Forbearance** is restraint from acting, withholding response by overlooking a provocation. Some writers also use this word in the sense of a kind of patience with tolerance in the face of trial and tribulation.

*Forbearance* is an international marriage of a solidly English stem, *forbear*, plus a purely French ending, *-ance*. It is rare that a word ending on *-ance* isn't derived from an adjective ending on *-ant*, like *importance* from *important* and *fragrance* from *fragrant*. The combination of the two origins of this word only adds mystique and intrigue to its phonetic luster. The verb *forbear* is irregular: *forbear, forbore, forborne*.

The softness of the sound of this word underpins the gentleness of its sense: "Linda, I beg your forbearance on this one occasion: I will never forget our anniversary again." Successful everyday living demands much forbearance of us all: "Edward seriously underestimated the amount of forbearance required in bringing up his children."

This lovely word was derived from the verb *forbear*, the descendant of Old English *forberan* "to endure," consisting of for "forward, through" + beran "to bear." The prefix *for-*, or *fore-*, also emerged as the preposition *for* in English, related to German *für* "for." The same original Proto-Indo-European root became per "through, for" in Latin. The root underlying *bear* also appears in most Indo-European languages. It may have originally referred to childbearing, since the alternative meaning of this word is "to carry a burden." (*Burden* and *birth* are both derived from *bear*.) In Latin it emerged as ferre "to carry," whence English borrowed it in a host of words like *refer, fertile, ferry, and differ*.

# Fugacious ∽ *Adjective*

**Pronunciation:** fyoo-**gay**-shus

**Fugacious** means fleeting, fleeing, running away, passing quickly. To botanists it means withering and falling off early or very soon.

English has a handful of absolutely lovely adjectives with meanings almost synonymous. *Fugacious* implies passage, movement past the viewer. *Ephemeral* has a similar meaning but implies only briefness of existence. *Evanescent* suggests vapor, a vague existence that is short-lived. The adverb of *fugacious* is *fugaciously* and the noun, *fugacity*.

Our lives are aswim in things that come and go, so this word comes in quite handy, "If my salary were only less fugacious, we could go out more often." Sightings are often fugacious: "He lived on fugacious glimpses of her face until the sight of her roused his pluck enough to ask her out."

*Fugacious* comes from Latin fugax (fugac-s) "fleeing, fleeting" from fugere "to flee," the verb in the phrase tempus fugit "time flies." It is akin to Greek pheugein "to run away." The original Proto-Indo-European root was *bheug- with that funny [bh] sound ([b] with a puff of air) that became [f] at the beginning of Latin words. (Latin fornix "oven," the source of English *furnace*, came from the same root as English *burn*.) *Bheug-* also went into the making of Sanskrit bhuj "bend" and German beugen "to bend."

# Furtive ∽ *Adjective*

## Pronunciation: furt-iv

**Furtive** means surreptitious, shifty, secretive, stealthy in an attempt to hide something either innocently or feloniously.

The sound [fur] is spelled several different ways in English: *fur*, *fir* and, in some dialects, *for* and *far* (which we do not encourage). So, we must remember that this word begins with the word for soft animal hair and not the evergreen tree. The adverb is *furtively* and the noun is created by the very commonplace suffix -*ness*: *furtiveness*.

This word may be used with positive or negative overtones. Furtiveness can imply a cover-up of improper behavior: "Calvin worried about the furtive dealings between his friend, Murray, and a shady character he met at the race track." It may also imply the cover-up of a perfectly innocent enterprise: "Mom noticed none of the furtive preparations for the surprise birthday party going on at the house."

This word was purloined from the French version of Latin furtivus "stolen, purloined." (Well, the word itself was asking for it.) By the time Latin had become French, this word was French *furtif* (masculine) and *furtive* (feminine); English helped itself to the latter. The Latin original came from furtum "theft," from fur "thief." No, this word has nothing to do with the fur trade but is related to Latin ferre "to carry," since thieves are known for carrying things off. The original Proto-Indo-European root, *bher- "to carry," descended though the Germanic ancestors of English to end up here as the verb (to) *bear*, and the nouns *burden* and *birth*, as mentioned earlier.

# Gambol ✁ *Verb, intransitive*

## Pronunciation: gæm-bul

To **gambol** is to frolic playfully, to leap or jump about joyfully. It brings me visions of children and baby animals skipping about playfully, though it covers any kind of play or simply relaxed meandering in gay spirits.

The sense of this word and, just maybe, its spelling makes it prettier than its homophone, *gamble*. But beauty can fade and the beauty of this lovely word is, indeed, fading even as I type this. Consider this page an alert and use this word more often to keep it gamboling about our vocabulary. In the United States we no longer double the final L when adding suffixes like *-ed* (*gamboled*), *-ing* (*gamboling*), and *-er* (*gamboler*) but doubling is encountered widely outside the US.

Gamboling is certainly more the prerogative of the young and lithe-legged than of their staid mature elders: "Claxton loved to watch his grandchildren gamboling in the backyard over the sunny days of summer." But gamboling adults are not unheard of by any means, "Gamboling crowds jammed traffic for hours after the home team won the championship."

This word is an adaptation of French gambade "skipping or frisking about" from Italian gambata "kick." This noun is based on gamba "leg," the Late Latin word for "hoof." It is also the origin of the English slang term gam "leg" and is a close relation of the French jambe "leg." The ending *-ade* apparently was confused with another suffix, *-auld*, which later lost its final D, resulting in gambol rather than *gambade*. (No, *gamble* is unrelated; it comes from *game*. By the way, it is better to gambol than gamble in Las Vegas.)

# Glamour ❧ *Noun, mass*

## Pronunciation: glæ-mur

**Glamour** is an allure arising from a combination of beauty, fashion, elegance, and style.

The English word for "glamour" is itself glamorous, though we must be careful spelling this word. It was borrowed from French with the ending *–our*, an ending still preferred in British English for words such as *behaviour*, *arbour* and *tumour*, spelled *-or* in the United States (*behavior*, *arbor* and *tumor*). But *glamour* retains *-our* in all dialects of English. The adjective, *glamorous*, on the other hand, is spelled everywhere without the U, probably to avoid repeating OU.

This is a word for conveying the enchanting quality of truly beautiful women: "Marigold possesses a genuine glamour of her own that doesn't require any cosmetic amplification." While *glamour* is not used to describe men, it can be used to depict things other than women: "The glamour of Hollywood attracts the superficiality from around the world."

You have probably long noticed that truly glamorous women speak grammatically. Well, glamour resulted from a Scottish mispronunciation of the word *grammar*! Glamorous women were originally "gramarous" in Scotland. In the Middle Ages *grammar* was the name of a witch's manual for casting spells called a *gramery*, a book about spelling of a different sort. Later the Scots changed the pronunciation of this word to *glomery* and soon came to use in reference to the magic spell itself. Since beauty itself may be spellbinding, it is no surprise that the meaning slipped over to enchanting beauty. The most Scottish Scot of all, Sir Walter Scott, first spelled this word *glamour*, bringing it down from the highlands in novels so compelling that the rest of the English-speaking world had to accept it.

# Gossamer ❦ *Noun*

**Pronunciation: gah**-suh-mur

**Gossamer** is the small threads spun by baby spiders as they hatch in late summer and that carry them through the air to their new lives wherever the gossamer sticks. However, it may also refer to anything extremely sheer, filmy or flimsy; possessed of lightness and softness approaching nothingness.

Since this word originally referred to the faint filament spun by baby spiders, a flimsiness barely visible, use this word sparingly. *Gossamer* is a mass noun with no plural form but it may be used as an adjective meaning "made of gossamer." The actual adjective, *gossamery*, carries the meaning "like gossamer," as a gossamery veil.

Keep in mind that this word retains its association with threads: "She brushed a bit of gossamer from her face with a gesture so gentle and graceful as not to damage it." It refers to lightness and sheerness at the very edge of visibility. As Cole Porter put it in his 1935 song, *Just One of those Things*: "It was just one of those nights, Just one of those fabulous flights; A trip to the moon on gossamer wings, Just one of those things." We can easily imagine sprites and fairies flying on gossamer wings.

This word is a smoothed-over version of Middle English gose-somer "goose-summer," which appeared often in the phrase "a goose-summer thread." A goose-summer was an Indian summer, a hot stretch in the fall when gossamer threads tend to drift about. The goose month (German *Gänsemonat*) is November, the time when geese are at their fattest and best for eating. There is a semantic connection with German *Sommerfäden*, Dutch *zomer-draden*, and Swedish *sommartråd*, all meaning "summer thread(s)."

# Ⓗalcyon ❧ *Noun, Adjective*

## Pronunciation: hæl-si-un

The **halcyon** was a mythical bird of ancient Greece that nested on the seas, calming them with magical powers until its eggs hatched. Today it is used most widely as an adjective reflecting calm, tranquil, placid states like that of the seas when the original halcyon was nesting.

The spelling of this Greek word is unusual for English so that prefixing or suffixing it would be difficult. There is a sponge, called *alcyonium* because it is remindful of the halcyon's nest. It has an adjective *alcyonic*. However, *halcyon* may be used as an adjective without suffixation, so an additional suffix would be redundant. Remember that the CY in the middle of this word sounds a lot like SI but isn't spelled that way.

When we think of total relaxation, *halcyon* should rush to mind: "After a halcyon respite on a Caribbean lagoon, adjusting to the pernicious traffic of Los Angeles proved difficult for Sandy Beach." Calm and tranquility, of course, are found in many places other than the sea: "The halcyon expression on Linda's face let Wesley know that everything was right with her world."

This word is Greek halkyon "kingfisher, halcyon" with the K softened to the [s] sound and spelled with a C in Latin. This word apparently arose from a compound containing hals "salt, sea" + kyon "conceiving, being pregnant," the present participle of kyein "to conceive," vaguely remindful of the halcyon's habits. The root of *kyein* apparently goes back to a Proto-Indo-European root meaning "swelling" and, by implication, "hollow place," for it is phonologically related to the Latin adjective cavus "hollow, dug out."

# Harbinger • *Noun*

**Pronunciation: hahr-**bin-jur

A **harbinger** may be a messenger or other sign of things in the offing.

No, harbingers do not harbinge, though Walt Whitman does harbinge future US States in *Leaves of Grass* (II.16). Until the seventeenth century harbinge meant "to lodge." Today harbingers harbinger.

The robin is the traditional harbinger of spring in North America but other harbingers abound: "I hope that the new president is a harbinger of better things to come for our company." Harbingers need not be human or animal, though: "Well, I think that the flowers George sent Gracie are a clear harbinger of a budding romance."

Fasten your seat belts: the history of this word is a doozy. In the fifteenth century, a harbinger (or *herbengar* then) was someone sent ahead to arrange lodgings—a harbinger of arriving guests. This word was an alternate of herberger "innkeeper, provider of lodgings," borrowed from Old French *herbergeor*, from herberge "lodgings" (Modern French auberge "inn"). Now, before you shake your head and say, "Of course, another one from French," guess where the French got this word. The French borrowed it from one of English's Germanic ancestors, heriberga "lodgings," made up of heri "army" + berga "shelter." *Heri* went into the making of *harbor* in English. If *berga* reminds you of German Berg "mountain" (as in the ice mountains known as *icebergs*), it should. The meaning of this word expanded from "hill" to "fortress," while the verb from it, *bergan*, came to mean "to protect, rescue." Berga "shelter" came from this verb. Whew!

# Imbrication ❧ *Noun*

**Pronunciation:** im-bruh-**kay**-shun

**Imbrication** is the ordered overlapping of rows of carefully arranged objects, such as roof tiles or fish scales.

This handsome word was derived from the verb imbricate "to overlap in rows." It comes replete with a family of derivations like the adjective, imbricative "overlapping in rows." The verb itself may be used adjectivally in the same sense if we reduce the pronunciation of the final syllable, pronouncing it [**im**-bruh-kut] instead of [**im**-bruh-kayt]. Either adjective may be adverbialized by simply attaching -*ly* to the end.

Using this word metaphorically, we can compromise the sense of "rows," but not that of "overlapping": "The tubular imbrication of the bromeliad's leaves rose to a burst of pink petals as lovely as any orchid." We can also use this word where "ordered" is implied only in the loosest sense: "The bright yellow leaves lay around the trunk of the maple tree in a disheveled imbrication suggesting an enormous sunflower."

*Imbrication* came to us from Latin imbricatus "covered with (roof) tiles," the past participle of imbricare "to lay roof tile." This verb came from imbrex, imbric- "roof tile," interestingly enough, derived from imber "rain." The Latin word seems not to have found its way into any other English words, but it comes from the same Proto-Indo-European word as Sanskrit abhra "cloud, rainy weather" and Greek ombros "thunder storm." The Greek word turns up in several scientific terms referring to rain, such as ombrometer "rain gauge" and *ombrology*, the branch of meteorology that deals with rain and rain patterns. The Latin variant of the same word underlies English *umbrella*. Guess why.

# Imbroglio ∽ *Noun*

## Pronunciation: im-**brol**-yo

An **imbroglio** can be a confused tangle or mess. It can also be an embroilment, an entangled disagreement or a disagreeable entanglement.

Here is a word whose beauty arises from the play between spelling and pronunciation. It comes from Italian. The Italian letter for the consonant [y] sound is J, but it is used only at the beginnings of words like justicia "justice." Inside words Italian uses digraphs, double letters like [gl] and [gn]. Any time you see these digraphs in an Italian word, remember that the G is silent but a Y is pronounced after the L or N, as in *intaglio, seraglio,* and *lasagna.*

Most often we hear this word used to refer to entanglements of human relationships: "Both Nixon's and Clinton's presidencies were marred by imbroglios with Congress." We are free to use it metaphorically to refer to almost any kind of entanglement: "Verna's room was a symphony of disarray that reached a crescendo in an imbroglio of dirty clothes at the end of her bed." Or would that spoil such a lovely word?

This word was borrowed recently from Italian, who borrowed it from French embrouiller "to tangle, confuse." The French word is the prefix en- "in, up" + brouiller "to blur, stir up, make cloudy." In the French of Norman England, this word became broiller "to mix up, confuse," which led to the original meaning of *broil,* "to brawl." In fact, *brawl* is just a more recent spelling of Old English, *broil.* The French creation of *brouiller* was based Vulgar (street) Latin *brodum,* a copy of an Old Germanic word that ended up in English as *broth.* (*Broil* in the culinary sense was borrowed from French brûler "to burn.")

# Imbue ✎ *Verb, transitive*

## Pronunciation: im-**byoo**

**Imbue** began its life meaning "to soak, saturate" and retains that meaning in the dyeing industry today, as to imbue a fabric with a deeper hue. Today, however, this word is used most widely in the metaphoric sense of suffusing or endowing thoroughly with a quality or property, as to imbue with patriotism or imbue a poem with life.

Here is a very short word containing two lovely consonants, M and B, and hiding the lithe glide sound [y]: the makings of a patently lovely word in English. It is easy to confuse this word with imbrue "to soak; to stain." *Imbrue* doesn't imply quite the thoroughness of the soaking that *imbue* does and *imbue* doesn't suggest staining in the pejorative sense as does *imbrue*. We may be imbued with a love of country (not imbrued) but we are imbrued (stained) with the guilt of our misdoings.

We are imbued with things that affect us deeply: "Imbued with her perfume and laughter, Rupert proceeded to ask Meredith to marry him." Objets d'art may be imbued as well as people: "Hermione imbued her bucolic paintings with a feminine perspective of the countryside where she had grown up that had never been seen before."

The origin of this word remains a bit hazy. It would seem obviously related to Latin imbuere "to moisten, wet, stain," but the evidence supporting this supposition is not at all robust. The French word imbu "imbued" arose about the same time as English *imbue*. Later the word imboire "to imbue, drink in" was 'backformed' from *imbu*, since *bu* is the past participle of boire "to drink." But the two words were not originally related.

# Incipient ✒ *Adjective*

**Pronunciation:** in-**si**-pi-unt

**Incipient** is an adjective that refers to things just beginning, just now detectable, in a formative stage, as an incipient love affair.

This word is a lexical gem with nouns just as lovely as it is. We have our choice of *incipience* or *incipiency*, depending on how many syllables we need. Even with all the hissing, it is a lilting word, considerably more fetching than its near synonym, *beginning*. The adverb is *incipiently*.

We often hear of incipient diseases and incipient species (those just showing enough differences to be separated), but incipience is all around us: "Marissa talks so well out of both sides of her mouth we suspect there may be an incipient lawyer lurking inside her." Incipient troubles are more easily solved than those in advanced stages: "We may have an incipient trouble-maker in the office: someone dumped a bottle of vodka in the water cooler today." (Some may think this person a morale-booster, though.)

*Incipient* comes by way of Latin incipien(t)s "beginning," the present participle of incipere "to begin," based on in- "in" + capere "to grab or take." The Latin verb *capere* also lurks inside the words *capture* and *captivate*. The original Proto-Indo-European root was *kap- "to grasp, grab." In German it became haben "to have" and in English, *have*. It is also related to words like *heave*, *hefty*, and *heavy*, qualities of things we tend to grab. We also have a word haft "handle of a tool or weapon," something we all grasp, even though the word today isn't what it used to be.

# Ineffable ∾ *Adjective*

**Pronunciation:** in-**ef**-uh-bul

If it is **ineffable** it is indescribable, inexpressible; it cannot be expressed in words. This word also has a narrower meaning: unspeakable, taboo, forbidden to be spoken, as the ineffable name of the all-powerful, omniscient One.

This word is the negation of effable "utterable, pronounceable," which has recently slumped into desuetude. The reason seems clear: all the words we utter are so utterly effable, when would we need this word? It is the unutterable words like *floccinaucinihilipilification* for which we need such a descriptive term. Since we avoid such terms, we seldom need words like *ineffable*. For this reason its meaning has shifted to either "indescribable" or "forbidden to be spoken."

This word is more often used to describe the indescribable, rather than the unspeakable: "Frieda Livery has an ineffable *je ne sais quoi* about her that attracts men like moths to a flame." It can, however, still be used in that sense: "Since he accidentally scored the winning goal for the opposition, his name has become ineffable; they just refer to him only as 'H' down in the athletic department."

This word comes via Old French from Latin ineffabilis "unutterable," an adjective based on the prefix in- "not" + ex "out of" + fari "to speak." The past participle of *fari* is *fatum*, whose meaning migrated from "spoken" to "prophecy" to "doom" as it became Old French *fat*. We then borrowed it as *fate*. *Fari* also lies at the bottom of fabula "story (something spoken)," which the French compacted into *fable* before lending it to us. The present participle, *fans*, turns up in infans "not speaking," which English also borrowed in its French version as *infant*.

# Ingénue ∾ *Noun*

**Pronunciation:** ahn-zhe-**noo**

An **ingénue** is a simple, decent, though naïve young woman, wide-eyed and precious, especially as a woman's role on stage or screen.

This lovely word has a peculiar pronunciation because much of the French pronunciation has been preserved. It has an adjective, *ingenuous* meaning either "open, frank, guileless." It is often confused with ingenious "inventive, imaginative." We also have an antonym, *disingenuous*, meaning "slightly dishonest, devious, rather deceptive." Many confuse this word with *disingenious*, an adjective that would be the opposite of *ingenious* if it existed.

Ingénues have become a standard role on the stage and in movies: "Marilyn Monroe played the stereotypical blonde ingénue for years in US movies." However, this word came down from the stage many years ago: "Marjorie can act a very persuasive ingénue to get her way with her father."

This bewitching French word devolved from Latin ingenuus "freeborn, honest" before its adoption by English. The sense of "honest, open, naïve" accrued to *ingenuus* from the assumption that freeborn people, the nobility, are good, honest people— noble, in both senses of the word. The root, *gen-*, originally meant "to beget, give birth to," and is found today in many English words borrowed from Greek and Latin related to birth or creation, such as *generate*, *genus*, *genius*, *genuine*, and *indigenous*. We know that this root originally referred to birth because the same root emerged in Greek as gyne "woman," found in such English borrowings as *misogynist* and *gynecology*.

# Inglenook ❧ *Noun*

**Pronunciation: ing**-gul-nUk

An **inglenook** is a nook or corner beside an open fireplace. More broadly, it may be a gathering point by the fireplace or hearth of a home.

An inglenook is literally a nook by the fire for *ingle* is actually a fire rather than a fireplace. Often benches were placed by the hearth or *ingleside*, so that conversations could be warmed by the home fire. Such benches were called *inglebenches* in and around Scotland in days gone by. An inglebred person is a homebody, someone who does not wander far from hearth and home.

Today, any cozy spot by a fireplace serves as an inglenook: "Lois loves to snuggle up with a good read in her warm inglenook on chilly rainy winter days." Actual nooks around the fireplace may serve a variety of function besides comforting folks: "Gloria's new house has inglenooks on either side of the hearth for the mementos she has collected on her trips around the world."

As already mentioned, this word comprises ingle "fire(place)" + nook "corner, recess in a room." Most dictionaries trace *ingle* back to Gaelic *aingeal* "fire, light," admitting some phonetic problems with the etymology. Another possibility, however, is that *ingle* is a Scottish variation of French angle "corner," which was in the language two hundred years prior to the appearance of *ingle*. *Nook* is another word that seems to have appeared mysteriously in Scotland and northern England with the same meaning it has today: "corner, wall recess." Attempts to associate it with Danish nokke "hook" and Dutch snook "pike" have run into obvious semantic problems.

# Insouciance ❧ *Noun, mass*

**Pronunciation:** in-**soo**-see-unts

**Insouciance** is an affected nonchalance, a blithe if not cheerful indifference, an emotional aloofness.

This soft, sensuous word is so fresh from French that some still prefer to give it the French pronunciation: [æN-su-**syahNs**], where the capital Ns mark preceding nasal vowels, vowels pronounced through the nose. This noun possesses all the beauty of the whispering breeze it sounds like. It is even more mellifluous than the adjective underlying it, *insouciant*, from which it is derived by simply replacing the T with CE.

Insouciance may be an indifference that borders on snobbery: "Reginald accepted his award with the aplomb and insouciance befitting the heroic figure he assumed himself to be." However, it may simply refer to a casually indifferent, unemotional attitude toward anything: "Madeleine had exhibited a consistent insouciance toward religion since Mr. Wright, the assistant pastor at her church, ended their affair."

The adjective from which this lovely word emerged comprises in- "not" + souciant "troubling," the present participle of soucier "to disturb, trouble." *Soucier* is how Latin sollicitare "to bother, annoy," turned out in French. *Sollicitare* itself was picked up by English and slashed to *solicit*. *Solicitare* was originally a compound based on sol- "single, whole" + citus "moved, summoned," the past participle of ciere "to move, stir, shake." *Sol-*, too, is found in many English words borrowed from Latin and Romance languages: *solid, solo* (via Italian), and *solitary* among them. *Citus*, of course, is the ultimate source of *cite* and *citation*.

# Inure ∾ *Verb*

**Pronunciation:** in-**yoor**

**Inure** means to so accustom or habituate someone to something to the point that they become jaded and ignore it. It usually appears as a past participle (*inured*) constructions without subjects, as to be inured to the glitter of high society.

*Inured* is a sophisticated alternative to *jaded*. We are inured of a thing when it brings us ennui, that sophisticated form of boredom achieved only by highly intelligent experienced, well-read folks. The state of being inured is inurement.

Inurement results in a dullness from overexposure, as this couple has experienced: "Hilda and Sterling Silverman were in danger of becoming inured to their marriage, so they set off to Paris in an effort to rekindle the romance that led them to the altar." Inurement often sets in at the office: "Matilda finally became inured to the drudgery of her job and survived only by adding little innovations of her own to brighten her workday."

The verb *inure* is a back-formation from *inured* "customary." That is to say, it was really an adjective mistaken for a past tense verb, so that a new verb, *inure*, was extracted from it. The adjective *inured* came from an old legal phrase *in ure* "in use, at work." *Ure* is a reduction of French oeuvre "work," found today in English *hors d'œuvre*, literally, "outside of work" in French. This word is the French descendant of Latin opera "works, labors," the plural of opus "(a) work" as in *magnum opus*. This Latin word was associated with wealth, for we find it at the bottom of *opulent* from Latin opulentus "wealthy, rich." Again, English copies the same word from French and Latin each time it changes.

# Ꝓabyrinthine • *Adjective*

**Pronunciation:** læ-buh-**rin**-theen

This most alluring inhabitant of the English vocabulary refers to anything that is bewilderingly convoluted, confusing, or maze-like. **Labyrinthine** also carries overtones of hopeless entrapment, of an inescapable situation.

*Labyrinthine* is the adjective accompanying the noun *labyrinth*. Be careful spelling both these words for they contain two traps. First, it has a Y and an I, in that order, which are easily transposed if we aren't careful. Second, this word often falls victim of syncope, the omission of the Y altogether. Remember to pronounce all four syllables of this word and keep the Y before the I.

Do use this word as much as possible as pure verbal decoration for all your conversations: "Somewhere amongst the labyrinthine passageways of my mind I have her name dutifully stored but for the life of me I cannot fetch it now." It is a word suggestive of the serpentine: "He laid out an argument for rearranging our cubicles that was so labyrinthine no one could determine whether it made any sense."

The history of this enchanting word, appropriately enough, is as mystifying as a labyrinth itself. English simply docked the E on French *labyrinthe*, itself a modest reduction of Latin *labyrinthus*, borrowed from Greek labyrinthos "maze, large building with intricate passages." The best guess (and it is just a guess) is that the Greek word came from the non-Indo-European Carian word labrys "double-edged axe," the symbol of royal power at the time. This would make sense as the name of the Minoan Palace on the isle of Crete, whose amazing maze of passages would have allowed the meaning of this tantalizing word to drift over to "a maze."

# Ꝉagniappe ❧ *Noun*

**Pronunciation: læn-yæp**

A **lagniappe** is a bonus gift added to a customer's purchase in gratitude for his or her business. This original sense invited its broadening to mean any bonus or extra value of any kind.

As mentioned before, look out for the pronunciation of GN in words from Romance languages like Italian and French; they are often pronounced [nyuh], as in *lasagna*, *cognac*, and *poignant*. Add *lagniappe* to that list. It was borrowed directly from the 'Cajun' French of Louisiana. In his *Life on the Mississippi* (1883) Mark Twain wrote, "We picked up one excellent word—a word worth traveling to New Orleans to get; a nice limber, expressive, handy word, *lagniappe*."

This word is a great way to impress others with the depth of your vocabulary: "Pat Agonia is so nice, Dad; she gave me a puppy as a lagniappe for taking one of the kittens!" Nowadays, any unexpected bonus passes muster as a lagniappe: "Ally would have enjoyed the picnic even if her boss hadn't fallen into the creek but that was a lovely lagniappe for tolerating him week in and week out."

Although the spelling of this word places its immediate origin in Louisiana French, that language in fact borrowed it from American Spanish la ñapa [nyahpah] "the gift." Spanish la "the" is derived from Latin illa, feminine of ille "that." The same pronoun is also the origin of French *le* and *la* which also mean "the." In fact, English *the* originated as an unaccented variant of the Old English ancestor of *that*. The origin of the noun *ñapa* is even more interesting. It comes from *yapa*, which means "additional gift" in the South American Indian language, Quechua, from the verb yapay "to give more."

# Lagoon ✎ *Noun*

## Pronunciation: luh-**goon**

A **lagoon** was originally a shallow bay protected from the open sea by a sandbar or coral reef or a lake inside a coral reef. Later it came to mean any lake connected to a larger body of water. Today it is grossly misused to refer to artificial holding pools for waste liquids, sludge, or sewerage.

This word has literally fallen from grace into the smelliest of sewers. It began its life as a centerpiece in our dreams of a tropical paradise. It was a dreamy place like the *Sleepy Lagoon* in Lawrence and Coates' 1940 song: "A tropical moon, a sleepy lagoon...and you." Today it is more likely a holding pit for pig and sewerage wastes, whose odor turns us blue. (Oh, the bestial things we do to our language!)

Let's float our minds as far away from the mess pig farmers are trying to make of this sumptuous word and focus on a sleepy blue lagoon like that pictured in the songs, surrounded by palm trees, and a punctual breeze that arrives just when the temperature becomes annoying. "Phil built his house on a shallow lagoon in a bird sanctuary so as to awake each morning amid a feast for eye and ear."

This word comes from either French *lagune* or Italian *laguna*. Both these words comes from Latin lacuna "pool, hollow, gap," itself a variant of lacus "lake," the word that gave English, well, *lake*. Related words are Greek lakkos "cistern, pond" and Gaelic loch "lake, pond," as in Loch Ness or Loch Lomond. Russian luzha "pool, puddle" is also connected. Here is another word that provided a lexical bounty for English, which fed on it repeatedly over time: *lake, lacuna,* and *lagoon*—all from the same Latin word.

# 𝕷anguor ❧ *Noun, mass*

## Pronunciation: lӕng-gur

**Languor** is a melancholy lack of vigor and vitality, a lethargy of mind and body, as from heat or humidity. It can also convey a sense of woeful inertia, a mildly sad gravitation to stillness, quiet.

This word belongs to a family of words with a motley assortment of suffixes. *Languorous* is directly related to the noun while its cousin, *languid*, expresses less melancholy. A languid mood is one absent motion or motivation; a languorous one is also woeful and a bit romantic. The verb is *languish*, which carries an even stronger sense of sadness; to languish implies mild desperation at being trapped in a situation with little or nothing to do.

Anything that dissuades us from activity produces languor: "Buck Shott's natural repugnance to physical labor was well suited for the languor that settled in over his farm in summer." Otherwise, this word implies wistfulness and just the hint of regret: "William Arami has been foundering in a deep languor ever since Mary Dagai refused his proposal of matrimony." The languor of a cool, windless summer evening is familiar to all of us who live in the country.

While heat-induced languor may cause your tongue to hang out, this word is unrelated to French langue "tongue," the origin of *language*. *Languor* comes from Latin languere "to be weak, faint." This verb would seem to come from the Proto-Indo-European root (s)leng- "weak, slack," which came directly to English (unborrowed) as *slack*. The parentheses around the S indicate that it is a Fickle S, disappearing in some languages, not in others. The N could also be parenthesized, since it was also lost along the way to English. Indeed, neither the S nor N shows up in another Latin word from the same root: laxus (*lak-s-us*) "lax, slack," whence English *lax*.

# Lassitude ☙ *Noun, mass*

## Pronunciation: lӕs-uh-tyood

**Lassitude** implies lethargy, torpor, listlessness, a lack of energy, spirit, or vitality. It can also refer to simple apathy, a lack of interest in something in particular or things in general.

Although this word approaches the sense of *lethargy*, *torpor*, and *listlessness*, it is not the same. Lethargy is a drowsiness that interferes with alertness. Torpor is a deeper drowsiness, right on the edge of sleep or unconsciousness. Listlessness suggests more of a disinclination to move or be active rather than a change of mental state. Lassitude is more of a lack of motivation to act. Taken together, though, these words provide a nice little lexical toolkit for dividing inactivity into several more precise senses.

Hot weather often affects us in the direction of lassitude: "The tropical heat brought out a certain lassitude in everyone, driving them inside to commune with the air conditioner for most of the day." You can, however, find other motivations behind lassitude: "The overbearing personality of the manager spread a lassitude over the shop that sapped all interest in the job from employees." *Molassitude* would be the slowest sort of lassitude—if it were only a word!

*Lassitude* was copped from Old French which inherited it from Latin *lassitudo*, the noun from adjective lassus "weary." This word is based on a stem (las-) that goes back to Proto-Indo-European *le- "let go, slacken" plus a suffix -*d* (*led*-), that also gave English *let* and *late*, not to mention German lassen "let." With the ancient suffix -*n*, it pops up in Russian as len' "laziness," Latvian as lens "slow," and Latin lenis "soft, gentle," which is also at the bottom of English *lenient*.

# ℒeisure ∽ *Noun, mass*

## Pronunciation: **lee**-zhur (US), **le**-zhur (UK)

**Leisure** is a period when we are free from work and other responsibilities, a time to rest, relax, or otherwise engage in relaxing activities.

The sound [zh] as in *fusion, pleasure,* and *leisure* is a pleasant sound and the R in the suffix *-ure* adds to the luxury of this word's sound. *Leisure* is used a lot in adjectival contexts, as in *leisure activity, leisure suit,* but it is only a noun used as a modifier in these instances. Remember that this word is usually pronounced differently in the US (**lee**-zhur) than it is elsewhere in the English-speaking world (**le**-zhur). The UK pronunciation has slightly more allure than the US alternate.

This lovely word is often used redundantly with *time*. Leisure is, of course, a period of time, so *leisure time* is redundant: "Rachael Grace spent most of her leisure hiking, camping, and picnicking along the Appalachian Trail with Geoffrey." Even should we work two jobs, when we are not at work, we are at leisure: "Cy Andrews builds exquisite hand-tooled furniture in his shop in his leisure."

English borrowed this word from Norman French *leisour,* which acquired it from Old French *leisir* "to be permitted." Old French inherited its version from Latin licere "to be permitted," the source of English *licit* and its more frequently used negative, *illicit*. The present participle of this Latin verb is *licens, licentis* "being permitted, allowed," which English also uses as *license* "undue freedom," as well as a permit to do something. English not only borrows words voraciously, time and again we see how it borrows the same word repeatedly at different stages of its development.

# ℒilt ❧ *Verb, intransitive*

## Pronunciation: lilt

*Lilt* is first and foremost a musical word meaning to speak, sing or play music in a light and lively, pleasantly cheerful manner. It is probably used more often to refer to light, bouncy movements, as though dancing to music.

An English word spelled the way it is pronounced is a rarity but that is what we have here. This authenticity only adds to its beauty. It supports an identical noun that allows you to walk with a lilt or speak with a lilt in your voice. Feel free to use the participle as an adjective: a lilting air played on a xylophone could be heard in the background.

Lilt is usually a quality seen or felt in sounds or motions: "When Gloria Size noticed her boss at a table across the restaurant, she immediately lilted over for a chat." Almost any motion is lovelier with a lilt: "Pietro was swept away by the lilt of Angelina's hair as she casually descended the stairs."

This beautiful little word left too few crumbs to follow back to its origin. Someone suggested that it might be related to Dutch lullepijp "bagpipe." This may be true but it doesn't tell us anything about its origin. It is also most probably related to *lull* and *lullaby*, but that doesn't help us either since we don't know where either of these came from. We may have to give up hope of finding an explanation of this word and simply enjoy the beauty of the way it is today.

# 𝔏issome ∽ *Adjective*

## Pronunciation: lis-um

Someone who is **lissome** is supple, slender, gracefully limber and agile afoot. You would expect a lilt in the gait of a lissome person.

*Lissome, lithesome,* and *lithe* all share pretty much the same meaning not unexpectedly because they are variations of one and the same word. More on that further on. If you don't like the E at the end of this word, ignore it: *lissom* is just as good a spelling as *lissome*. This adjective does come replete with an adverb and noun: those slender enough can walk about lissomely (or lissomly) as a result of their lissomeness (or lissomness).

*Lissome* implies movement facilitated by slenderness and flexibility: "Grace had grown into a charming, lissome teen-ager who leapt across the stage in her tutu effortlessly." This word refers to slender things but it implies motion: "Ages ago, when I was winsome and lissome, I could dance the limbo under a rod only two feet above the floor."

This word reflects remarkable indecision in the minds of English speakers over a particularly long period. The original word was *lithe* [laidh] (coming up next), which was first extended for no apparent reason to *lithesome* [laidh-sum] and then reduced to *lissome*, perhaps because *lithesome* was taken as a lisp. All this occurred with little change in meaning. The original stem shows up in some languages related to English with a Fickle N, as we see in German lind "soft, dulcet" and Latin lentus "soft, pliant, tough."

# Lithe ❧ *Adjective*

**Pronunciation:** laidh

**Lithe** objects are gracefully slender; supple, flexible, easily bent or flexed, as a lithe willow withe. However, like *lissome*, it may also refer to anything graceful in movement, bending supply and appealingly, as a lithe dancer.

I hesitated including this word having just written that, historically, it is the same as the preceding word, *lissome*. However, today it is a different word with a very slightly different meaning: *lithe* refers more to bendability even though it may serve as surrogate for *lissome* itself. This word, as mentioned earlier, has a synonymous variant, *lithesome* which, for some reason known only to my ear, I prefer: a lithesome dancer lilting fragilely across the stage. The comparative and superlative forms of this word are lither and lithest, and the noun is litheness.

Not surprisingly, the meaning of this word is itself quite lithe, making it easily adjusted to a wide range of situations: "Phillipa Byrd was accustomed to uttering phrases so lithe they could fit any position on an issue." When you think of subtle flexibility, this should be one of the words that come to mind: "Amanda was as lithe slipping in and out of conferences at the office as she was in moving across a dance floor."

This word is another with a Fickle N, an [n] sound that comes and goes for reasons that still escape us. The original PIE root was something like len-t- "soft, loose." Old English líðe "mild, flexible" eschewed the [n] while German kept it in lind "gentle, soothing, dulcet." Latin also retained the [n] in its adjective lentus "pliant, flexible" while Russian kept the [n] but not the [t], producing in len' "slowness, laziness."

# ℒove ✌ *Noun, Verb*

**Pronunciation:** luv

**Love** is a deep affection and respect for someone or something. However, it can also refer to a sexual passion. Finally, for reasons that will become clear further on, it also means "zero, nothing" in tennis scoring.

If you play tennis, you have had the occasion to use *love* frequently. This lovely word is used in scoring tennis matches, where it has the unfortunate meaning of "nothing, zip, zilch, nada." Tennis scores are love, 15, 30, 40, game, rather than 0-1, 2, 3, 4, win. A tie is a deuce, possibly because players exclaim that when they tie.

The first two meanings of this word remind us that there is an easy 'love' and one that requires concentration: "Falling in love is easy; converting that kind of love into the long-term sustainable variety is much harder—a labor of love." The first kind doesn't last as long or run as deep: "Phil Anders is a man who loves to love; he just doesn't quite know how."

Today's lovely word started out in Old English as *lufu* but, thank heavens, like many of us, it improved with age. It is based on a root with sticking power: we see the signs of it in German *Liebe*, Russian *ljubov*, and Latin *libido* "pleasure." There once was a time when "love it or leave it" would have been redundant, since *leave* comes from the same parent word. "By your leave" once meant "by your pleasure," since *love* is associated with pleasure. Though we have no hard evidence, the tennis term may well be the English rendition of French l'œuf 'the egg', in a sense akin to English *goose egg*. The shift to *love* would be the natural result of folk etymology, the conversion of an unfamiliar foreign word into a recognizable one in the native language.

# Luxuriant ❧ *Adjective*

**Pronunciation:** lug-**zhUr**-i-unt

Things **luxuriant** are rich, thick and abundant in growth. They may be densely overgrown, so profuse as to send chills down the spine. *Luxuriant* can also mean lavish, plush, profusely ornate in design and execution.

*Luxuriant* is but a tad more sightly than *luxurious*, but it bears the implication of a rich thickness that we do not sense in its fraternal twin. *Luxuriant* is derived from the verb *luxuriate* while *luxurious* clearly comes from the noun *luxury*. The unsightly X in this word is saved by its pronunciation which is not the usual [ks] that we hear in *ibex* and *crux*, but a much more luxuriant [gzh].

The first thought *luxuriant* brings to mind is a luxurious thickness: "Cassandra's luxuriant hair plummeted down her back and ended in a thought of coiling but without quite bringing itself to do so." This word does incorporate a sense of luxuriousness, however: "The vaulted interior of the mosque was covered with luxuriant, artistic Arabic script based on the *Qur'an*."

This alluring word was taken from Latin *luxurian(t)s*, the present participle of *luxuriare* "to be luxuriant, to luxuriate." The Latin verb came from luxuria "excess, luxury," which evolved into Old French *luxurie*. Middle English snapped this one up with its original Latin sense of "lust, lasciviousness." If we go back a step further, we find Latin luxus "dislocated, dislocation," used figuratively in the sense of "excessive" and implying excess that is misplaced, abnormal. This word came from the same Proto-Indo-European word as English *lock* (of hair). So to speak of someone with luxuriant locks is to speak, etymologically, that is to say, redundantly.

# 𝓜ellifluous ❧ *Adjective*

**Pronunciation:** me-li-floo-us

We use **mellifluous** most often in speaking of speech itself, specifically of pleasantly beautiful, highly articulate, even poetic speech. Less often, it is used in the sense of sweet as honey or even sweetened with honey.

This word amply demonstrates how we often conflate the senses. As we will see below, *mellifluous* originally referred to honey flowing over the tongue but now it refers more often to the sweetness of speech than to that of taste; in other words, speech as beautiful as honey tastes. It has a synonymous cousin, *mellifluent*, with an equally beautiful noun, *mellifluence*.

This word is itself one of the most mellifluous words in English; it is almost onomatopoeic. The image it conjures up is that of a smooth flow of speech approaching if not reaching poetry: "Rhoda Book's rich, mellifluous prose attracted as many readers to her work as the poignant stories she told with it." This term describes the ultimate goal of the translator: "The interpreter translated each sentence into mellifluous, idiomatic English that literally dripped from her tongue."

This word is the English makeover of Latin mellifluus "dripping with honey," based on mel "honey" + fluere "to flow." Latin *mel* and Greek meli "honey" come from the same root as French and Spanish miel "honey." English and Russian replaced the final L with a D, producing Russian med "honey" and English mead "fermented honey." *Flu-* is a cognate of English *flow* and *flu*. The latter is a clipping of Italian influenza "influence," from the days when diseases were believed to be the evil influence of celestial bodies. By the way, Greek *meli* also underlies melissa "honey bee," quite a fetching name for girls these days.

# Moiety ∽ *Noun, mass*

**Pronunciation: moy**-uh-tee

A **moiety** is a half or other share of something and a word for those interested in a lovelier way of saying "part" or "share." Anthropologists hold it to be either of two tribes related by unilateral descent from a common ancestor.

Vowels are always more beautiful than consonants; in fact, as we have remarked before, the most beautiful consonants are those most similar to vowels. Well, there is no question why this word is beautiful: the heart of it is a rare three-vowel cluster. In the plural, *moieties*, two more are added. It is much more fetching than synonyms like *shares, halves*, and *parts*.

*Moiety* usually refers to one of two parts: "Sharon's moiety in her father's estate was materially larger than she had anticipated." The advantage of *moiety*, though, is that it may also refer to one of two parts that are not equal: "Moira was happy to find out that her moiety from the divorce settlement was much larger than Marshall's."

*Moiety* is another word whose ancestors changed so much over time that English was able to borrow them repeatedly for a raft of new words. English captured *moiety* from French moitié "half," a reduction of Late Latin *medietas*. This word was reworked from medius "middle," the neuter singular of which is *medium*. An odd little fellow that shares the same source as all these words is *mullion*, the post separating double windows. It began as Anglo-Norman moienel "middle," a descendant of another adjective from *medius*, Late Latin medialis. Somehow, the L and N switched places (metathesized) before settling on the spelling *mullion*.

# 𝕸ondegreen ∾ *Noun*

**Pronunciation: mahn**-duh-green

A **mondegreen** is a word or phrase that results from a slip of the ear, a reanalysis of a phrase, such as the fabled child's reanalysis of "gladly the Cross I'd bear" as "Gladly, the cross-eyed bear."

*Mondegreen* is an accidental creation, so we wouldn't expect to find derivations from it. It is a common misconception that this word is limited to the mishearing of song lyrics. Mistaking *Guantanamera* in the song of the same name with *one-ton tomato* certainly is a mondegreen. Mondegreens, however, occur wherever people speak and listen.

Over my career I have seen and heard of many mondegreens in freshman essays. One freshman referred to the Spanish classic *Don Quixote* as *Donkey Hote*. Well, as many freshmen know, it's a 'doggy-dog' (*dog-eat-dog*) world in which we shouldn't take anything 'for granite' (*granted*). My all-time favorite, however, came from a colleague across the hall, who came into my office one day, barely in control of her laughter, to show me a freshman composition about a person with a 'devil-make-hair' (*devil-may-care*) attitude toward life.

A good deal of the beauty of this word comes from its history. It first emerged in the title of an essay about slips of the ear by Sylvia Wright "The Death of Lady Mondegreen," published in *Harper's Magazine* in November 1954. In this essay Wright tells about mishearing the final line of the Scottish ballad "The Bonnie Earl O'Murray," which reads, "They hae slain the Earl Amurray, And Laid him on the green." Wright always (mis)heard the last two lines as "They hae slain the Earl Amurray, And Lady Mondegreen." No one has come up with a better name for these slips of the ear.

# Murmurous ⌇ *Verb, Noun*

**Pronunciation: mur**-mur-us

A murmur is a low, soft, indistinct, continuous sound, or speech in a subdued voice suggestive of discontent or bad news. Murmurs may imply complaining in hushed tones. **Murmurous** is the adjective for both these senses, it means to resemble or be filled with murmuring.

The noun *murmur* enjoys the best of two linguistic worlds. It is a French borrowing that has been all but completely assimilated into English, so we may use the English form, *murmuring*, as an adjective or noun, even convert it into a native adverb, *murmuringly*. *Mumurish* and *murmurless* are also at our disposal. But then we also have the full panoply of Romance suffixes, including *murmuration* and this adjective, *murmurous*, the most alluring of all due to its repetition of the Ms and schwas (the [uh] sound) and its transparent reflection of its meaning.

When describing the sounds of nature, this word bears only positive connotations: "Benchley slept best to the music of murmurous waves lapping against the shore in front of his beachside bungalow." When referring to human speech, however, it cannot escape a suggestion of the pejorative: "There was murmurous prattling wafting through the office about the boss's dalliance with his research assistant."

French *murmurer* "to murmur" is one of dozens of similar words in western Indo-European languages with the same meaning, including German *murmeln*, Portuguese *murmurar*, Italian *mormorare*, all related to Latin *murmurare*. The word is clearly onomatopoeic, but it wasn't the Romans who first created it. Sanskrit marmara "rustling" and Ancient Greek mormurein "to roil" indicate that this word came to us from Proto-Indo-European with little change along the way.

# Ρemesis ✦ *Noun*

**Pronunciation: nem**-uh-sis

A **nemesis** is an undefeatable archenemy, an unconquerable opponent. More recently nemeses have become almost any danger or threat to well-being or, finally, simple retribution, revenge, or punishment.

English words ending in *-is* [is] form their plurals by replacing this suffix with *-es* [eez], so the plural of this word is *nemeses*. Similar words include *basis*, *crisis*, and *analysis*. *Nemesis* is another lexical orphan. *Nemesism*, aggression turned against oneself, enjoyed a brief existence in the field of psychology of the 40s and 50s but, like so many other things, didn't survive the 60s.

Mystery lovers will recall Moriarty, the archcriminal who was the nemesis of Sherlock Holmes. Agatha Christie's last novel around the character of Miss Marple was called *Nemesis*, a title taken from a comment by a character in a previous novel, who saw her as an indefatigable enemy and avenger of crime. It was inevitable that someone would name a chocolate dessert "chocolate nemesis," since the urge for chocolate is an undefeatable threat to our well-being that punishes those who surrender to its temptation with undesirable gains.

This word comes from the Greek nemesis "indignation, retribution," also the name of the Greek goddess of retribution, Nemesis. The noun comes from the verb nemein "to allot," related to German nehmen "take" and Old English niman "to seize, take." Although the Old English word didn't make it through to us, we see remnants of it in *nimble* and *numb*. The former originally meant "quick to seize," while the latter was the past participle of *niman*, meaning "taken, seized," as by a cold or other disease.

# Offing ✎ *Noun, mass*

**Pronunciation: aw**-fing

The **offing** is that area of the sea off shore but still visible, just beyond anchorage. This sense has been extended to cover the immediate future, used almost exclusively in the phrase, in the offing, meaning occurring soon, imminent, at hand.

The crystallized phrase "in the offing" has virtually erased from our collective memory the original sense of this word, one of the most beautiful in the language. It is even more beautiful for being purely English and not deftly lifted from a foreign patois that brushed against English in the past. It is an orphan without links to other words except the preposition-adverb *off* that you see lurking in its root.

The beauty of this word lies in its sound and the sea air that inhabits it. It is the perfect playmate for another beautiful word, *lagoon*: "Beryl and Wellington lounged casually by the sleepy lagoon, their eyes lazily following a trim old schooner slipping past in the offing." Were only such a respite in the offing for me!

It is rare to find nouns derived from adverbs or prepositions but this word is exceptional in this respect too. *Off* started out as a variant of *of* just as that word became a preposition. *Off* remained an adverb for centuries and only recently became a preposition itself, e.g. "Dad just fell off the porch, Mom" (not "off of," as when it was an adverb). *Of* and *off* come from an interesting family, the black sheep of which is *offal*, slaughterhouse waste. Most peculiarly, however, the word *puny* is a distant relation. This word is a corruption of French *puisne* from puis "then, later" + né "born," plus the assumption that children born later are weaker. Now, French *puis* is the great-grandchild of Latin post "after, later" that comes from the same word *apo* that also produced English *of* and *off*.

# Onomatopoeia ✎ *Noun, mass*

**Pronunciation:** ah-nuh-mæ-duh-**pee**-yuh

The status of a word whose pronunciation imitates its meaning: *buzz, crack, clink, clank, clang, fizz, thump, hiss, sizzle,* and *slurp* are all words reflecting **onomatopoeia.**

English has very few words with four vowels in a row. The greater appeal of vowels than consonants in English words buys *onomatopoeia* a ticket to the top of the most beautiful list. We haven't yet decided how to spell the adjective; both *onomatopoeic* [ah-nuh-mæ-tuh-**pee**-ik] and *onomatopoetic* [ah-nuh-mæ-tuh-po-**et**-ik] are at your disposal.

All languages sport onomatopoeic words. English has *thud, meow, quack, tinkle, boom, squeal,* and *mumble,* in addition to those mentioned above. These are all words referring to sounds made by imitating the sound itself. The words for the sounds that animals make are almost always onomatopoeic. *Moo, cheep, cock-a-doodle-do, gobble, quack,* and *caw* serve to demonstrate the point.

This word was blatantly traced from Greek *onomatopoeia,* the abstract noun from onomatopoios "name-maker." This word is a compound composed of onoma(t)- "name" + poiein "to make." *Onoma* comes from the Proto-Indo-European root (o)nomen- "name" with a fickle initial O that came and went over the course of Indo-European language history for no apparent reason. The word came to German and English as *name* and to Russian as *im(en)ya.* We find a variant, *onym,* in many English words, such as *pseudonym* (false name), *anonymous* (nameless), plus *synonym, antonym, eponym,* and several others.

# Opulent ⁊ *Adjective*

**Pronunciation: ah**-pyuh-lunt

To be **opulent** a thing must be sumptuous, luxurious, reflecting great wealth and richness, or have plush, luxurious appointments. This word is also used to express great size or number for it can mean "thick or dense with."

The fact that English has more words like, *plush, luxurious, posh,* and *sumptuous,* referring to wealthy lifestyles than words referring to poverty reflects the aspirations of the English-speaking world as its economic status. *Opulent,* though, is used more often to refer to luxurious hair, plush upholstery, sumptuous greenery, and opulent dogwoods than monetary richness. *Opulent* may be used adverbially with the appropriate suffix, *opulently,* and the noun is formed by replacing the final T with CE: *opulence.*

Opulence first and foremost describes luxurious surroundings: "Jason Rainbows lives on an opulent yacht docked where he can make a quick getaway should investigators discover how he paid for it." Figuratively, however, it refers to any sort of superabundance: "Tiffany Lampe was known more for her opulent coiffures than those opulent candlelight dinners."

This word made its way to us from Latin opulentus "rich, wealthy." It is based on the noun opus "work," which we use in English as a stand-alone word and also as a root in words like *opera* and *operate.* The adjective comes from a suffixed form *op-en-ent-* that became *opulent-* by way of 'dissimilation,' one of the linguistic means of avoiding sound repetition in a word. Latin didn't like the *en-en* syllable combination in *openentus* and so replaced the first *en* with *ul.* (Please don't ask why.)

# Palimpsest ❧ *Noun*

**Pronunciation: pæ**-limp-sest, puh-**limp**-sest

A **palimpsest** is a document written on a sheet or paper or parchment that has been used before, the earlier writing either covered over or still partially visible. Anything with more than one layer or aspect beneath its surface, anything multilayered, may be called a palimpsest.

Not all Americans agree with the usual pronunciation of this word, the first one at the top of the page. It is most widely pronounced [**pæ**-limp-sest] with the accent rather unnaturally on the initial syllable. Many now shift the accent to the antepenultimate syllable [pah-**limp**-sest], where it is more comfortable. It is difficult to hear the [p] because it is so similar to the [m]. Notice how both are pronounced by closing the lips. Try to keep the P when uttering this word but don't despair if it eludes you.

This word effortlessly settles into the description of almost any work of art: "*The Little Prince* is much more than a children's story; it is a palimpsest of the author's affairs, stormy marriage, and perhaps even a covert suicide note." Places or people whose history shows through a modern façade beg for it: "The neighborhoods of New York are a palimpsest of all the cultures that passed through Ellis Island in bygone years."

This word goes back through Latin *palimpsestus* to Greek palimpsestos "scraped again." In Greek it was a compound containing palin "again" + psen "to rub or scrape." Greek palin derives from Proto-Indo-European *kwel-/kwol "turn," the same root underlying Latin collum "neck" and English *collar*. *Psen* is akin to Sanskrit psati "eat" and Russian pisat' "write," both originally specialized types of scraping.

# Palisade ❧ *Noun*

**Pronunciation: pæ-**luh-sayd

A **palisade** is a line of pales (pointed logs) serving as a fence or defensive wall. In the plural (*palisades*) it usually refers to a stretch of high cliffs along a riverbank or overlooking a lake.

The intimation of palaces underlies the beauty of this word, especially when it refers to the cliffs along a river. Keep in mind, however, that we use only the plural to express this sense: the Palisades are the highlight of the Hudson River.

A palisade is a labor-intensive means of defense: "Dewey Rose built a sturdy palisade around his garden to keep out the rabbits but he underestimated the bounding power of his adversaries." Palisades along a river or lake are just to be enjoyed: "The palisades along Split Rock Creek in South Dakota are so majestic Jessie James vacationed in a cave there for several days after his robbery of the Northfield, Minnesota bank."

This good word is French *palissade* touched up very lightly. It comes from palissa "stake" + -ade, a suffix often referring to groups (*brigade, parade*). *Palissa* is a remnant of Late Latin *palicea* from Latin palus "stake." The ultimate root was pa(n)g- "fasten" with our old friend the Fickle N, sometimes there, sometimes not. It does not appear in *palus* or in *pact*, which comes from Latin pacisci "to agree," nor pax "peace," often the result of a *pact*. *The* Fickle N did invade the Germanic languages where we find German fangen "catch, capture, seize" and English *fang*, the pointed object by which animals seize things.

# Panacea ❧ *Noun*

**Pronunciation:** pæn-uh-**see**-uh

A **panacea** is a remedy for everything, for all problems or difficulties; a cure-all, a catholicon.

Pandora, whose name means "all gifts," was the first mortal woman according to one version of Greek mythology. Zeus gave her the gift of a box that, when opened, allowed all the ills of humanity to escape. Since Pandora's box created the immediate need for a panacea, it should surprise no one that this word comes from Greece (more below). The English adjective from this word is *panacean*, as a panacean remedy or a panacean approach.

Since the times of the ancient Greeks, we have come to know much more about illness, enough to know that there is no single cure for all of them. However, outside medicine the idea persists. Many think a tax cut will be a panacea for all economic problems. Others have thought nuclear bombs a panacea for all international conflicts. We each have our own idea of a panacea for all our problems: "Buffy, a tattoo and a nose ring are not a panacea for your dating problems."

This word is the undisguised Latin noun, *panacea*. It referred to an herb Romans believed could cure all diseases. The Romans traced their copy from Greek panakeia "universal cure" from pan "all" + akos "cure." Greek *pan* appears in *Pandora*, already mentioned, and in *Pandemonium*, the all-demon city in Milton's epic poem *Paradise Lost*. It is productively used to create adjectives like *pan-Arab*, *pan-African*, *pan-American*, a clipping of which, *Panam*, underlies the name of Panama.

# Panoply ∾ *Noun*

**Pronunciation: pæn**-uh-pli

*Panoply* originally referred to a full suit of armor, implying a sense of completeness and protection. It was easily extended, therefore, to the sense of a full array of anything, especially if used for protection, as a panoply of excuses.

We need to be careful not to confuse this word with *canopy*, also a protective covering of sorts. Avoiding that trap, we may use this word to refer to a full array of anything or any protective covering. "Having a panoply" is expressed by the adjective *panoplied*, as a panoplied position in government, a position protected from adversity and adversaries.

The senses of a full array and protective covering blend together in some instances: "The lawn was languishing under a panoply of recently descended leaves a panoply of fall colors." Since *panoply* means "full array," it doesn't need modifiers like *full* or *complete*: "He presented a panoply of arguments for his position that no one present could rebut."

This mellifluous word is the English makeover of Greek *panoplia*, built out of pan "all" + hopla "arms, armor," the plural of hoplon "tool, weapon." Little to no evidence of the Greek prefix pan- "all" appears in other languages. It does appear widely in English words borrowed from Greek, such as the one on the preceding page, *panacea, panorama*, an "all-view," *pandemic*, a disease affecting all people, and *pantheon*, originally a shrine dedicated to all gods. *Hoplon* is another word we find little evidence of in other languages. The only clear relative is Latin sepelio "to bury," which underlies sepulchrum "grave, sepulcher," and which is the origin of English *sepulcher*.

# Pastiche ❧ *Noun*

**Pronunciation:** pæ-**steesh**

A *pastiche* is an artistic work composed of random pieces or parts lifted from the work of others. It can, in fact, be almost anything composed of diverse or incongruous parts or style, a motley medley, a hodge-podge collage.

This word is a delicate piece of conversational embellishment that must be used with proper attention to the disparity between the spelling of CH and its pronunciation as [sh]. A pasticheur [pæ-stee-**shoor**] is someone accomplished at pastiching, even if they are not daring enough to use this word as a verb.

This word is most frequently used in referring to creative works that are mixtures of materials or styles: "The movie *Chinatown* is a pastiche of film noir, historical documentary, and mystery." If we look around, we find ourselves surrounded by pastiches, so we have ample opportunity to use this very decorative term: "The neighborhood Cecilia lived in was a pastiche of every European culture plus a few from the Far East."

This exquisite child of the English lexicon is the French version of Italian *pasticcio*, a pie of mixed ingredients or, figuratively, a mess or imbroglio. Both the French and the Italian inherited the word from Vulgar Latin pasticium "pastry," which also went into the making of French pâtisserie "pastries, pastry shop." The Latin word is based on pasta "dough," and is still alive and kicking in Italian. Portuguese, and Spanish. English borrowed the word at least three times: as *pasta* and *paste* before French removed the S from it, and as *pâté* after. The hat (circumflex) over a vowel in French usually indicates that a Latin S has been eliminated.

# Penumbra ❧ *Noun*

**Pronunciation:** puh-**num**-bruh

A **penumbra** is a demishadow or the edge of a shadow that is still shady but brighter than the center, especially the shadow (umbra) of an eclipse. By extension, it may also be used in reference to the outer region of anything that is not as pronounced as the center, a gray, transitional area.

This word is very liberal in its production of derived forms. It sports two adjectives, *penumbral* and *penumbrous*—take your pick. You may also take your pick of the plurals; *penumbrae* and *penumbras* are at our disposal. It is a very relaxed word, indeed a cool word, as might be expected of a word that is always in the shade.

Between eclipses, this word is used mostly to refer to metaphoric demishadows: "Vadim made every effort to prevent Beryl's falling into the shadow of his gregarious personality, but still she felt herself somewhat in his penumbra." Anywhere *shadow* might fit but we need to imply a soft or slight shadow, remember this word: "Reston worked hard to keep his reputation from falling under even the slightest penumbra of doubt."

New Latin *penumbra* is based on Latin paene "almost" + umbra "shadow." That *umbra* is the same one you see in *umbrella*, a device originally designed to protect lovely European ladies from the rays of the sun. We also find it in *umbrage*, which now means "offense" as much as "shade," as does its lovely adjective umbrageous "shady; offensive." *Paene* can also be found in penultimate "next to last" as in the penultimate syllable of a word. We also see it in *penultimatum*, the threat of an ultimatum so popular among parents of small children.

# ℗etrichor ↔ *Noun, mass*

## Pronunciation: pe-truh-kor

**Petrichor** is that distinctive pleasant fragrance of rain falling on dry ground. It is produced by oily, yellow-gold globules, rather like perfume, that come from organic matter that collects in soil.

This exquisite word unleashes a bouquet of pleasant undertones: of pets and petting, chords and choruses. It was introduced by two Australian geologists, I. J. Bear and R. G. Thomas, in a 1964 article that appeared in *Nature* magazine, referring to a rather specific aroma. However, we have all experienced the pleasure of the smell of rain against dry earth, and now we have a word to explain that pleasure. It is too young to have progeny yet, but when it reaches appropriate seniority, I predict it will produce an adjective, *petrichoric*.

This word certainly belongs in the vocabulary of all terroirists, who believe the soil affects the flavor of wine: "I'm certain that the bouquet of this chardonnay comes from the petrichor of the soil where the vines grew." But once we are comfortable with it, we can release our metaphoric creativity, "Her entrance into his life was a refreshing petrichor ending a long season of dry relationships."

It is amazing how such a beautiful word can arise from such a distasteful combination as *petrichor*. It comes from the root of Greek petros "stone" + ichor, a mythical rarified fluid that flowed in the veins of the gods. *Petros* is also the Greek form of the name "Peter," which is why Jesus claimed his disciple Peter to be the rock on which His church would be built. So the name of the film character, Rocky, is simply a translation of the Greek *Peter*.

# Plethora ❧ *Noun*

**Pronunciation: ple**-thuh-ruh

**Plethora** originally referred to an excess of blood in the body, thought to cause a ruddy complexion and possible puffiness. Today, however, this word refers to an abundance if not superabundance of anything: much, many, a profusion.

Most dictionaries today concede that this word can refer to merely an abundance of something; however, as the reference to blood shows, it originally referred to an excess. The line is between much and too much, but is a very fine one—at what point do we have too much money or chocolate? The plural of this word is *plethorae*, as in a *plethorae* of flowers and chocolate. *Plethoras* is occasionally used, too, though either plural of this word is passing rare. The adjective is *plethoric*, pronounced either [**ple**-thuh-rik] or [pluh-**tho**-rik].

The world today is faced with a plethora of problems created by overpopulation and global warming. However, plethorae are also found at home: "Mom, please don't ask another thing of me: I have a plethora of tasks that I must complete before going to bed tonight!" Doesn't every teenager talk like that? Plethorae also turn up in politics: "Bob Taille has such a plethora of volunteers for his political campaign that he doesn't need me."

This word comes to us via Latin from Greek plethora "fullness," the noun of pleos "full." The same root turned up in Latin with a suffix -*n* as plen-us "full," which wound up in English as both *plenty* and plenary "full, complete." After adding its own -*n* suffix, Russian reversed the order of the L and vowel (metathesis) to get polnyi "full." English metathesized the L, too, played around with the vowel, and added its own suffixes to produce both *full* and *folk*.

# Propinquity ∽ *Noun*

**Pronunciation:** pruh-**ping**-kwi-tee

A **propinquity is** nearness in time or space, proximity in any sense of the word, including propinquity in personality, kinship, thoughts, or style.

Be sure to avoid confusing this word with propensity "inclination", a false cognate often mistakenly substituted for *propinquity*. *Propinquity* comes with a plethora of adjectives, including *propinquitous, propinquous, propinquial, propinquant, propinquate,* even *propinque.* The first of these seems the most popular these days. Not much else can be found along the lines of related words.

Whatever you do, remember that this more elegant surrogate for "nearness" does NOT refer to an inclination—that's a *propensity*: "Chef Field has a propensity for overeating that is aggravated by his propinquity to the tasty edibles he prepares at the cafe." *Propinquity* refers strictly to proximity: "The propinquity of the teacher undermined the effectiveness of Morris's cheat sheets." Keep in mind, though, that the proximity may just as well be abstract as concrete: "The propinquity of their ideas about gardening led to a series of pleasant lunches in—where else?—their gardens."

English found this word begging to be snitched in Old French. Old French *propinquite* was inherited from Latin propinquitas "nearness, vicinity," the noun accompanying propinquus "near." This word, in its turn, is an extension of prope "near," whose comparative propior "nearer" and superlative proximus "nearest" underlie several other words English has appropriated, including *proximity, approximate,* and *appropriate,* all of which imply nearness to something.

# Pyrrhic ~ *Adjective*

**Pronunciation: pir**-ik

Capitalized, *Pyrrhic* refers to a victory or accomplishment whose cost outweighs its rewards. As an uncapitalized noun, **pyrrhic** refers either to an ancient Greek military dance, called the pyrrhic, performed in full battle array, or to a metric foot in poetry made up of two unaccented syllables.

This engaging word is used almost exclusively in the crystallized phrase "Pyrrhic victory," but as we will see below, this is not its only use. With a small initial letter, this word has a noun, *pyrrhics*, referring to the dance or the metric foot.

Pyrrhic victories often win the battle but lose the war. However, the use of this word is not limited to this fixed phrase: "Allowing Leticia to win the state salad-making finals was a Pyrrhic act of integrity by Leonard, since Leticia still refused to accept his proposal of marriage afterwards." Any small success that does not lead to a larger, related one is Pyrrhic: "Finishing the project ahead of schedule left Reynaldo with a sense of Pyrrhic accomplishment, knowing that he would be laid off anyway."

This lovely if short word has an eponym rather than a history. It was originally the name of Pyrrhus (318-272 BC), a Greek king of Epirus who fought the Roman Empire. He defeated the Romans twice, once at Heraclea in 280 BC and then again at Asculum in 279 BC. However, he suffered such losses in these battles that in *Plutarch's Lives* he is quoted as saying, "One more victory like this will be the end of me." Pyrrhus is also credited with the invention of the pyrrhic dance. Perhaps his battles would have fared better had he studied the battlefield more and the dance floor less.

# Quintessential ❧ *Adjective*

**Pronunciation:** kwint-uh-**sent**-chul

That which is **quintessential** contains the essence of the essence, the very heart and soul of something. A quintessential object may also be the perfect example of its class.

This adjective comes from the noun, quintessence "the most essential part." Although rather long, spelling this word is straightforward: simply add *quint* to *essential* and remember that it refers to the essence of the essence of anything, the most critical, defining quality of all such qualities.

The most common use of this extraordinarily beautiful English word is to identify a perfect example: "Itzhak Perlman is the quintessential violinist." A word this beautiful finds applications everywhere: "Anna Mallory is such the quintessential animal lover she won't even wear Naugahyde jackets because she doesn't want the naugas to suffer."

This word is a compound based on Medieval Latin quinta "fifth" + essentia "essence." The fifth essence in medieval philosophy was the substance of which the heavenly bodies were composed. It was also supposed to be present in all things, so that one of the major objectives of alchemy came to be the extraction of the quintessence by distillation. *Essence* comes from Latin essentia "essence" from essens "being," a noun derived from the verb esse "to be." The essence of a thing was seen as its core being which, when it came to humans, often referred to the soul.

# Ratatouille ✌ *Noun*

**Pronunciation:** ræ-duh-**too**-ee

**Ratatouille** is a vegetable stew made of eggplant, zucchini, tomatoes, peppers, and onions, prepared in or with olive oil, though these ingredients vary from chef to chef.

French borrowings that have not been assimilated into English usually sound beautiful to English ears, a prejudice probably going back to Norman England when the French ruled our ancestors. This good word, however, sounds a little facetious due to its similarity to *rat-a-tat-tat*, the onomatopoetic word for the sound of a machine gun. So facetious it is, in fact, that the Disney Corporation used this word as the title of a feature cartoon that attempts to extend the cuteness of Mickey Mouse to rats.

This word is arcane enough that the subtitle of the Disney film is a pronunciation guide for the title: *Ratatouille* (Rat-a-too-ee). However, the dish is delicious when properly created, so its name should be more popular: "If you aren't busy tonight, why not pop over to my place and I'll throw a little ratatouille together."

*Ratatouille* began as a blend of French ratouiller "to disturb, shake" and tatouiller "to stir." *Tatouiller* is a repetitive alternative to touiller "to stir, mix," the descendant of Latin tudiculare, a verb built up from *tudicula*, the name of a machine used for bruising olives. *Tudicula* is the diminutive of tudes "hammer," hence "a small hammer." The same French *touiller* was allured into English some centuries ago to toil away as the English word *toil*.

# Ravel ❦ *Verb, transitive*

**Pronunciation: ræ-vul**

To ravel may mean to entangle, to knit or weave together. However, it may just as well mean the opposite: to disentangle, to fray, to unweave!

Richard Lederer calls words like *ravel* contranyms, words that are their own antonyms. Originally, *ravel* meant only "to entangle," but today it also means just the opposite: "to disentangle, to fray, or unknit." Keep in mind that *ravel* may also be used as a noun in the sense of a tangle, as when combing the ravels out of someone's hair.

Now that *unravel* relieves *ravel* of its negative meaning, lets focus on the positive meaning of ravel: "Wyatt Hertz had raveled his personal affairs into such an entanglement that he couldn't sort them out with the help of two therapists." As you can see, this word works well metaphorically: "Tommy's former friends took little time to (un)ravel the mystery of who put the vodka in the punch at the church social."

*Ravel* is unrelated to the raveling music of the French composer Maurice Ravel [ruh-**vel**]. It is a Germanic word that shows up only in Germanic languages and a few borrowings from Germanic elsewhere. Dutch rafelen "to entangle" and ontrafelen "to untangle" were the origins of both English verbs, verbs based on the noun ravel "a loose thread." The same Germanic root gave us the *raff* in *riffraff* via Old French raffer "to sweep together," also borrowed from Dutch *rafelen*. *Raffle* came from the same French verb. It originally was the name of a dice game that must have resembled sweeping the floor.

# Redolent ～ *Adjective*

**Pronunciation: re**-duh-lunt

Things **redolent** are strongly fragrant, aromatic; they have a strong, pleasant odor, as a room redolent of burning wood or a fresh bouquet. This adjective can also refer to things that are suggestive, evocative, arousing suspicion, as a decision redolent of politics.

*Redolent* and its noun *redolence* are beautiful to a large extent because of their association with an attractive color featured prominently in their root. *Redolence* differs from *fragrance* (which almost made this book) in two respects: it refers to a strong fragrance and it can also refer to a strong figurative smell arousing suspicion. An aroma is a particular or distinctive but always pleasant smell.

This word is used most often to refer to a pleasant physical aroma: "The living room was redolent with the needles of the Christmas tree that only stoked the children's excitement." It does emerge with the figurative sense of "smell suspiciously of," though: "Mama's suggestion that we put the children to bed early was redolent of self-interest."

This word goes back through Old French to Latin *redolen(t)s*, the present participle of redolere "to smell, to have an strong aroma." It is made up of re(d)- "intense" + olere "to smell of." This verb comes from Latin odor "smell," which English uses without disguise. Apparently, a suffix *-d* was added to *ol-*, causing the *-l* to disappear because Latin never liked the LD consonant cluster. Of course, olfactory "pertaining to the sense of smell" is composed of the same root + *fact(us)*, the Latin past participle of facere "to make, to do" + the English suffix *-ory*, itself made over from Latin *-orius*.

# Ɽiparian ⁓ *Adjective*

**Pronunciation:** ri-**pœ**-ree-un

**Riparian** describes the bank of a river, stream, lake or other body of fresh water. Why salt water is excluded beats me but fresh water ("sweet water" in French, Portuguese, Russian, and other languages) adds much to the allure of this word's meaning.

*Riparian* is as beautiful as the sound of the ripples lapping the river bank it implies. Writers have tried *riparial* and *riparious* in the same sense, but no other variation compares with the sheer beauty of *riparian*. Apparently, no one has attempted a noun from this adjective, leaving it to bask in its beauty alone.

Any time you are near a river, you can massage the conversation with this warm old lexical glove: "Every Fourth of July the village folk hold a riparian repast by the susurrous Susquehanna and spend the afternoon fishing, wading, and waving at the passing boats." Occasionally the kids catch a riparian frog, lazy from a nap in the shade. Deer, ducks, and other wildlife are often found in riparian scenes, slaking their thirsts and grazing on the lush grasses that grow there.

This word comes from the Latin adjective riparius "pertaining to a bank" from ripa "bank of a river or stream." The original pre-Latin word meant "to break or tear," as seen in its Swedish descendant, river "to scratch, to tear." It also went on to become *rift, river*, and *reef* in English, rif "reef" in Dutch and, in German, Riff "reef," a scratchy conglomerate on which you could rip your swimsuit if you aren't careful. Finally, English *arrive*, borrowed from French *arriver*, originated as Latin arripare "to reach shore", a verb derived from ad "(up)to" + ripa "bank, shore."

# ℞ipple ∽ *Noun*

**Pronunciation: ri-**pul

A **ripple** is a small wave on the surface of water that moves away from the disturbance that causes it. Generally, the wave is one of many circular such waves radiating outward from the source of the disturbance. This word is also used figuratively to refer to series of consequences, each one causing the next, emanating from in a single original incident.

Although we are examining the nominal side of this word, it may also be used as a verb, as a threat that rippled quickly through all departments. *Ripply* is the adjective meaning "having ripples," which opens the door for *rippliness*. The present participle, *rippling*, may also be used as an adjective or a noun indicating the process of rippling.

Visible and invisible ripples are things we usually enjoy seeing and feeling: "The sight of the ripples radiating from the spot where his fishing line entered the water sent ripples of pleasure through August Fischer." Larger entities are susceptible to ripples, too: "Susan Boyle's appearance on the *Britain's Got Talent* show sent ripples through the world of entertainment." Millions of people who heard Susan's voice felt emotional ripples rising to their eyes as they listened to it.

No one is sure where this word came from, which leaves us a broad latitude for speculation. *Ripple* should have something to do with ripping, as a handle is related to hands and a spindle is something used in spinning. However, the two words seem semantically too distant for a connection. Middle English had a word ripelen "to scratch" which might also be the source of *ripple*, but even if it were, we still do not know where that word comes from.

# Scintilla ॐ *Noun*

## Pronunciation: sin-ti-luh

A **scintilla** is basically a spark or small flash; however, this sense has been expanded to refer to a trace amount of anything, an iota.

The plural of *scintilla* is *scintillae*, though no one will laugh if you say *scintallas*. Don't be bumfuzzled by the SC consonant cluster at the beginning of this word: both are soft and pronounced together as [s]. *Scintilla* brought a family with it when it came to English. The verb *scintillate* means to sparkle vibrantly, literally or figuratively. Scintillating conversation always delight us as much as scintillating fireworks.

We often use this word as a synonym for iota, "There isn't a scintilla of truth in anything Polly Graf says." However, remember it really refers to a spark, a spark of any kind: "Cyril didn't bring a scintilla of wit that might have brightened the conversation." Or pushing it just a bit further: "Consistency bored Dana; she much too much enjoyed the unexpected flukes and scintillae of life."

This absolutely resplendent word is Latin scintilla "spark," swallowed whole by English. Latin built *scintilla* from an ancient Proto-Indo-European word *skin(t)-* "to shine," which also went into the making of English *shine*. In German the root behind these words emerged as Schein "shine" and in Greek in skiron "white parasol." English *shine* has now been blended with *glimmer*, giving us *shimmer*, as well, a word whose meaning lies not far beneath that of *scintillate*.

# ⊚Sempiternal ↜ *Adjective*

**Pronunciation:** sem-pi-**tur**-nul

Eternal, everlasting, without beginning or end.

The question naturally arises: If we have eternal, why do we need this good word? This word simply emphasizes the fact of infinity or an extreme length of time in hyperboles. We may emphasize the idea of infinity in adjectival, adverbial (*sempiternally*), or noun form (*sempiternality*). "Why do you sempiternally ask questions?!" is more emphatic than the same sentence with eternally. Look out for the I in the middle of this word where you might expect an E.

Here is a dreamy example: "Ariel Greenpasture is a devoted potamophile, who enjoys stretching out along the riverbank and listening to the sempiternal flow of its waters." (Ariel, of course, is a river-lover who does not live in the US southwest, where her love of rivers would be nourished by streams that flow annually, not sempiternally). You will probably have more opportunities to use this word in hyperboles than in its literal sense: "The Bickertons' sempiternal quarreling got on everybody's nerves."

This word seems to have been around sempiternally. It comes to us via French from the Latin compound adjective *sempiternalis*, based on semper "always" (as in the US Marine Corps motto, semper fidelis "always faithful") + aeternus "eternal." *Semper* comes from a root meaning "as one, same, together" found in English *same*, Russian sam "self," Sanskrit sam "together," and Greek homo "same." *Aeternus* comes from the pre-Latin word aiwo-t- + the Latin time suffix, -ernus. The same word aiwo-t reached English through its Germanic ancestors as *aught*.

# Seraglio ❧ *Noun*

**Pronunciation:** suh-**ræl**-yo

During the Ottoman Empire a **seraglio** was that part of a Turkish palace where wives and concubines were secluded, the chambers of the harem. Today, it usually refers to any rich, luxurious oriental or Middle Eastern palace, especially one located in Turkey.

This is a word of unique beauty in sight and sound closely associated with women. It also evokes our sympathy as a lexical orphan with no verbal or adjectival relatives. Its beauty overpowers its dark history and encourages us to find figurative uses for it. Its plural is pure and simple: *seraglios*.

We could save the beauty of this word from its history by simply updating its usage: "I can remember how, as a child, I much preferred the seraglio of happy voices and sensuous perfumes in my grandmother's kitchen to the smoke-sodden company of the men in the living room." Women seclude themselves voluntarily these days in ways that tempt another figurative use of this word, "She was attracted by a seraglio of women escaping their husbands once a week to chat happily around a table by a window overlooking a garden."

This word is an almost perfect copy of Italian *serraglio*. It probably came from a Vulgar Latin word never recorded, serraculum "enclosure," which would have been derived from Latin serare "to bolt," a verb based on sera "door-bar, door bolt." The Italian word may also have been influenced by Turkish saray "palace" taken from Persian saray "inn." *Saray* may also be found in Russian today, meaning "barn." Do keep in mind that most of this is speculation.

# ⊚erendipity ∞ *Noun*

**Pronunciation:** se-ren-**di**-pi-dee

**Serendipity** is the pleasant discovery of something delightful while looking for something more mundane.

*Serendipitous* is the adjective for this noun and *serendipitously*, the adverb. A person given to serendipitous discovery is a *serendipitist* if you want to push the derivations that far. *Serendipity* is often slightly misused. Remember, for a discovery to be serendipitous, you cannot be looking for the object of the discovery but for something else.

Possibly the greatest act of serendipity was Columbus's discovery of the Americas while looking for the East Indies. It is not serendipitous that the cookbook you ordered arrives the day of the big dinner for your boss; that would be plain good luck. You must be looking for something else: "What serendipity! I went to Lionel's for a game of poker and met someone who offered me a job at twice my current salary."

This word comes from an ancient Persian fairy tale called *The Three Princes of Serendip*. According to the eighteenth-century British author, Horace Walpole, the tale was about three princes who "were always making discoveries, by accidents and sagacity, of things they were not in quest of." Walpole added the French suffix -*ity* in a letter written to a friend in 1754. Serendip was the former name of Ceylon, known today as Sri Lanka. It is the Persian version of Arabic *Sarandib*, borrowed from Sanskrit Simhaladvipa "Island where Lions Dwell." Sanskrit is an ancient language of India related to English. Arabic belongs to the unrelated Semitic language family, which includes Hebrew and Berber.

# Summery ⮾ *Adjective*

**Pronunciation: suh**-mer-ee

Things **summery** may be warm like a summery day or befitting summer, light or gauzy, like a summery dress. Anything suggestive of summer may be summery.

This lovely word that suggests a filmy fabric waving in a warm breeze is, of course, the adjective derived from *summer*. The noun *summer* has such a lilt to it that it attracted Shakespeare's attention in naming his light-hearted fantasy, *A Midsummer Night's Dream*. It even offers a poetic alternative to the word *year* in expressions like a boy of only eleven summers.

When I think of summery things, cottony shirts and dresses come to mind, the soft light clothing we wear when the temperature soars: "Julie wore a summery frock with a floral design that blended uncannily with the flowers in the garden where we held the picnic." If warm days may be summery, why not warm hearts? "Rachael always brings a summery smile to any conversation."

The ancestry of this word is ancient, though it seems not to have descended into Latin or the subsequent Romance languages. Some have rather unconvincingly suggested that its root, *sam-*, lies beneath the surface of some fish names in those languages. For sure *sama* in Sanskrit meant "half-year, season," while Armenian *amarn* and Zend *hama* both mean "summer," and all three words come from the same source. The word is very prominent in the Germanic languages, though, as demonstrated by German *Sommer*, Dutch *zomer*, Danish *sommer*, and Swedish *sommar*.

# Sumptuous ❧ *Adjective*

**Pronunciation: sump**-choo-wus

If it is **sumptuous**, it must be lavish and expensive, large and luxurious, and always opulent.

This word is onomatopoetic to the extent it is remindful of plumpness and sensuousness of a sumptuous venue. Here is a word sumptuously endowed with Us and Ss. The adverb matched to this adjective is *sumptuously* and the noun, *sumptuousness*. This word has no spelling pitfalls so long as you watch your Ps and Us.

This word is often used in discussions of entertainment: "Gilda Lilly served a sumptuous dinner on the verandah for her investment broker and his wife." What you wear to a sumptuous meal is fair game for this word, too: "Portia Radcliffe came to the ball in a sumptuous gown of taffeta and velvet, dripping in jewelry."

This plush billowy word comes from Old French *sumptueux* (Modern French *somptueux*), the lexical heir of Latin *sumptuosus*. This word was expanded from sumptus "expense," the past participle of sumere "to take, buy," used as a noun. *Sumere* was compacted from sub "(from) under" + em- "to take." This root picked up an initial N in Germanic languages and went on to become German nehmen "to take." In Old Slavic it became imeti "to have," which evolved into *imati* in Modern Serbian and *imet'* in Russian. We don't find evidence of it in English except in words borrowed from Latin like *example* from Latin *exemplum*, the noun from eximere "to take out," made up of ex "out" + emere. *Sample* came from the French rendition of the same word, Old French *essample*.

# Surreptitious ❧ *Adjective*

**Pronunciation:** suh-rep-**tish**-us

Whatever is **surreptitious** is stealthy, clandestine, secret, as surreptitious espionage activity. Taking pains to avoid being seen or noticed can also be surreptitious, as would be a surreptitious smile or glance at a party.

This is a much better word than any of the synonyms used in the definition above because it is long and slithery, full of hissing—all of which gives it a blithely sinister air that all contenders for its meaning lack. In fact, this may be why the adjective is often associated with deceitfulness, that and the fact that it sounds so much like *suspicious*. The adverb is *surreptitiously* and the noun, *surreptitiousness*, is even better with its extra round of hissing.

This word is not always associated with deceit, though it usually does raise suspicions and imply guilt, "Pat Downe's surreptitious glances at the neckline of Claude's wife forced Claude to cut in on them in the middle of the dance." Guilt, of course, is often accompanied by embarrassment: "At the reception for the ambassador, Rhonda casually raised her left hand to her face and, with her right pinky, surreptitiously removed something from her left nostril."

*Surreptitious* entered Middle English, more or less willingly, from Latin, which has a similar word *surrepticius*. This word is an adjective from *surreptus*, the past participle of surripere "to take away secretly," a combination of sub "(from) under, secretly" + rapere "to seize, grab." The Latin root *rap-* also underlies English *raptor*, *rapacious*, and *rapt*, a state of mild seizure. *Ravage* comes from the same root, smoothed by hundreds of years rolling off the tongues of French speakers, from whom we borrowed it.

# Susquehanna ❧ *Noun, Proper*

**Pronunciation:** sus-kwuh-**hæ**-nuh

The name of the longest river on the American east coast and the sixteenth longest in the United States and a major tributary to the Chesapeake Bay is also one of the most beautiful words in the English language—**Susquehanna**.

It would be possible to write up a hundred of the most beautiful words in English, all of which were borrowed from indigenous American languages. Many of these words refer exclusively to the American Indians themselves, such as *wigwam, squaw, papoose,* and *tomahawk.* Many that are firmly ensconced in the language are less than attractive: *muskrat, squash, caribou, chipmunk, hockey.*

Place names are another matter. Twenty-eight of the fifty US state names are taken from various American Indian words, not to mention countless names of mountains, rivers, cities, counties and regions. *Shenandoah, Malibu, Niagara, Nesquehoning, Tahoe, Mississippi, Mahanoy, Rappahannock,* and *Tallahassee,* all have alluring sounds in any language. The problem is that the vast majority of people don't know what they mean. As a result they become only labels identifying people and places, so the beauty of these words is limited to their sounds and personal associations.

*Susquehanna* is my favorite for I have lived on the banks of this beautiful river for more than forty years. This word probably came from the name of a small Iroquois tribe that once lived along its banks. The word for "big river" in Oneida, another Iroquois language, is *kayhuhowana,* from kayhuha "river" + -owana "big one." Unfortunately, the Susquehanna nation was wiped out in the mid-eighteenth century and no one noticed whether it had a similar word prefixed with *sus-*.

# Susurrous ✵ *Adjective*

**Pronunciation:** sU-**sU**-rus

Emitting whispering or rustling sounds makes anything **susurrous**. Breezes, brooks, or bacon sizzling in a frying pan all produce susurrous sounds

This Latinate word has more whispering sounds [s] than our native Germanic words, like *hiss* and *whisper*. As a result, it conveys the sounds of waterfalls, brooks, and breezes more invitingly. This word also lacks the negative connotations of hissing. If you don't like so many Ss, you may use *susurrant* in its stead. Just remember this important spelling rule: one S, two Rs and an O before the last U.

Streams and breezes are notoriously susurrous, which is why the banks of the Susquehanna are such a delightful place to live. However, this adjective also associates well with voices, "Miss Teak's susurrous voice drove men to distraction—some with lust, others with suspicion." Of course, leaves become susurrous when the wind rakes them in the fall, often striking up a susurrous banter with the sizzle of the grill.

This word comes from Latin susurrus "whisper," one of the most perfectly onomatopoeic words in any language. It is, in fact, an old Proto-Indo-European root *sur-* or *swer-* "sound," found in Sanskrit svirati "sounds" and Serbian svirati "to play (a wind instrument)." Reduplicating the first syllable of this root would give us the *susur-* that we see in the root of the Latin word. The same root, by the way, developed naturally through our Germanic ancestors to become *swarm* in English, another susurrous object we occasionally encounter.

# Talisman ⤳ *Noun*

## Pronunciation: tæ-liz-mun

A **talisman** is an object with magic powers, a charm to magically ward off evil and promote good fortune.

Unlike an amulet, a charm worn around the neck to protect against evil and promote good fortune, a talisman may take any form. The power of a talisman is talismanic and the person who carries a talisman, or believes in them, is a talismanist. The plural is *talismans* and NOT *talismen*.

Talismans are positively commonplace in our lives: four-leaf clovers, rabbits' feet, and other such charms are all talismans. Just apply your mind creatively: "Muriel's talisman is a locket with her mother's picture in it that she rubs before she makes any important decision." Men cling to talismans, too: "Marshall will never sign a contract with anything other than the pen he inherited from his father; it's like a business talisman to him."

*Talisman* is a world-class world traveler. It set out in life as the Greek word telesma "consecration ceremony," whose meaning shifted slowly to that of a statue protecting a temple. If we wish to trace *telesma* a little further back, we will find that it is based on telos "end, result, tax." We find this word in teleology "the study of natural design and purposes." Arabic borrowed *telesma* as tilsam "talisman" and tilsimani "one who deals in talismans." From Arabic it was borrowed back into the Romance languages as Spanish *talismán*, French *talisman*, and Italian *talismano*. English probably picked it up from French.

# Tintinnabular ❧ *Noun, mass*

**Pronunciation:** tin-tin-æ-byU-lur

**Tintinnabular** is the adjective derived from the verb *tintinnabulate* and means accompanied by the ringing of bells or resembling the ringing of bells.

Since the chime of bells is a pleasurable sound and this word was created in imitation of that sound, it was destined to be one of the most beautiful in the language. And so it is. The doubling of the second N is a nice touch. This adjective comes from the same source as the noun *tintinnabulation*, a fair maiden of a word itself.

Things tintinnabular ring and tinkle: "The tintinnabular greeting of the wind chimes in the garden was a constant invitation for Charles to stop and smell the roses." The ringing, of course, may be physical or metaphorical: "Nothing raised Gilliam's spirits more than the tintinnabular voice of his daughter meeting him at the door upon his return home."

Seldom do we find a more obvious example of onomatopoeia (the imitation of a sound in that sound's name). The 'tin-tin' built into this word is not far from English *ding*, *ding-dong*, and *ding-a-ling*—all onomatopoetic creations but burdened with connotations of silliness. The Romans seem to have been the ones who made it up, for it is difficult to find relatives in other Indo-European languages. Middle English snitched its word from Latin *tintinnabulum* "small, tinkling bell." *Tintinnabulum* was made from the verb *tintinnare* "to jingle," itself a reduplication of *tinnire* "to ring," the original onomatopoetic word lying way down there beneath the suffixal accoutrements. We also see it in the medical term *tinnitus* "ringing in the ears."

# Umbrella ⚭ *Noun*

**Pronunciation:** um-**bre**-luh, **um**-bre-luh

An **umbrella** today is a parasol affording protection from the rain and consisting of a pole with a usually round canopy that rises and collapses along it. Figuratively, it may refer to anything that 'covers' a variety of other things, as an umbrella festival that includes music, art, and crafts organizations.

*Umbrella* is a common but far from ordinary word. It begins humming UMB and ends in a lullaby of Ls, all of which lends this word a gentle softness. Umbrellas are essentially the same as parasols except that parasols provide protection from the sun while umbrellas provide it from the rain. Umbrellas are also known affectionately in some areas of the United States as 'bumbershoots.'

Let's begin with the original sense of this lovely little word: "Madeleine profoundly enjoyed sharing her umbrella with Malcolm on a rainy days." Now, Malcolm sits under an umbrella at work all day: his corporation is an umbrella organization for a diversity of companies purchased over the past twenty years.

An umbella in ancient Rome was a little shadow. This word contained no R despite the fact that it was the diminutive form of umbra "shade, shadow" (with an R). It was also the word for parasol or umbrella, both of which cast a small shadow. No one knows what happened to the R in the diminutive but by Late Latin, just before Latin broke up into French, Italian, Portuguese, and Spanish, the R was returned. The result was *umbrella*. English picked this word up from Italian *ombrella*, from Late Latin *umbrella* after the R had been returned under the influence of the original word *umbra*.

# Ⓤntoward ∾ *Adjective*

**Pronunciation:** un-**tord**

**Untoward** situations are those that are unfavorable, adverse, unfortunate. They may also be simply uncontrollable or unruly, out of hand. Untoward people or untoward actions are awkward, inappropriate, ill-suited or ill-timed. Untoward actions are usually embarrassing.

Here is a purely English word with an appealing sense of self derived from the fact that its meaning seems mysteriously disjoined from the way it looks. The base of this word is, oddly enough, *toward*, a preposition so unsettling used as an adjective that some folks add an adjective suffix, making it *untowardly*, along the lines of *friendly* and *womanly*. This form also serves as an adverb and provides a basis for a noun, *untowardliness*.

Untoward human behavior is behavior unsuitable or untimely for the given circumstances: "Bret was a great success at the party until he made an untoward suggestion about the age of the hostess." Still, this word can serve as a near synonym of *unfavorable*, too, as in: "Barnum is hoping to invest in the stock market but is waiting until the economic conditions are less untoward."

The components of this word are very obvious: *un* + *to* + *ward*, the same *ward* we find in *northward, leeward,* and *forward*. *Toward* began as a redundant compound preposition, since *to* and the suffix *-ward* have the same meaning, "in the direction of." However, as an adjective, it came to mean "what is about to be," as a toward storm. From there it slipped into the sense of "making progress," as a toward student. This led to the sense of "willing, obliging," whereupon its negative, *untoward*, came to mean "unwilling, unobliging," only a hop and a skip away from its meaning today.

# Vestigial ✄ *Noun*

**Pronunciation:** ves-ti-jee-ul

Anything **vestigial** is but a tiny surviving trace, a mark or indication left behind by something no longer present.

*Vestigial* is the adjective derived from *vestige*, a tiny surviving trace or reminder of something. The noun also went into the creation of the verb *vestigate*, which originally meant to follow the vestiges of something. The sense of the verb, however, eventually came to be the same as that of *investigate*, rendering *vestigate* moot and unnecessary.

This word is most often used to refer to suggestive aspects of something in ruins that leaves us with an impression of its previous life, "After fifty years of dissolute living, Farouk was but a vestigial shell of what he once had been." However, the term is too beautiful to be used only pejoratively: "The vestigial evidences of Carla's presence—the last iotas of her perfume disintegrating on the air, the lipprint on her wine glass, the memory of her voice—would have to suffice Frederick until the weekend."

This fetching bit of lexical treasure was captured from French during one of English's many forays into that language's garden of words. French inherited *vestige* from Latin vestigium "foot-print, trace," which seems to have come from nowhere (outer space?) It appears in at least one other Latin word, investigare "to track," whose past participle, investigatus "tracked," was easily converted into English *investigate*. There isn't another vestige of this word in any other Indo-European language that we can find.

# Wafture ～ *Noun*

## Pronunciation: wahf-chUr

**Wafture** is the motion of waves or the activity of waving. This includes the motion of a hand waving or something in the hand being waved. Finally, like the verb underlying it, this word may refer to floating or bobbing either on the waves or in the air.

The elegance of this noun comes from the verb *to waft*, as to waft gently on the waves or through the air. It implies gentleness and aimlessness, as a fisherman's float might waft along the surface of the lake or the fragrances of the garden might waft through the air. Both the noun and the verb are on the lexical endangered species list, but they are worth saving for their beauty alone.

Anything wavy is wafture: "The draft brought in a wafture fragrant with the scent of fallen leaves, reminding Natasha that the snows of winter were just beyond the hill." In fact, any waving motion qualifies: "The last suggestion of her elegance that Baldwin saw was the wafture of her hand bidding him good-bye as he entered his car."

Just as the meaning of this word suggests accidence, unintentionality, its history is something of an accident, too. It originates with *wave*, of course, but a peculiar pronunciation of it in northern England and Scotland: *waff*. This pronunciation is a holdover from Old English, where the word was *wafian*. By Middle English the F had turned to V everywhere but the northern dialects. The Germanic languages inherited this word from the Proto-Indo-European word for "weave"; in fact, *weave*, *web*, and *waver* all come from the same source.

# Wherewithal ∽ *Noun, mass*

**Pronunciation:** hwer-**with**-ul, **hwer**-with-awl

**Wherewithal** is means or strength to do something, more often than not the financial means.

*Wherewithal* is an odd little word, a lexical orphan with no derivational family. Withal "in addition, among other things" seems to be a relative but is only coincidentally composed of the same words: "Tryon Makepeace is withal an excellent negotiator," meaning that among his other talents, Tryon negotiates well.

*Withal* is a bit outdated but *wherewithal* is still very much alive around the English-speaking world; it most frequently refers to finances: "Gooden Small didn't have the wherewithal to buy the yacht he wanted, so he settled for a rather modest speedboat." This word may, however, be used to refer to strengths outside the realm of finance: "I don't think Lil Abner has the emotional wherewithal to survive another divorce."

English has a dying set of compound adverbs made up of *where* + a preposition in which *where* means "which." For example, the house wherein I reside means the house in which I reside. The tools wherewith to complete the job means the tools with which to complete the job. This makes sense with the original meaning of *wherewithal*: all with which (one needs to…). It is odd for an adverb to slip into the grammatical garb of a noun, but much stranger things have happened over the course of the history of the English language.

# Woebegone ~ *Adjective*

**Pronunciation: wo**-buh-gawn

**Woebegone** is a word that sounds, appropriately enough, a bit woebegone itself. People *woebegone* are people sad, melancholy, sorrowful, which is to say, woeful. This word may also apply to inanimate objects, in which case it means run down, ramshackle, in woeful condition.

There is little to say linguistically about today's word. It is not widely used any more, which allows Garrison Keillor of *A Prairie Home Companion* to use it as the name of his fictional hometown, Lake Wobegon, Minnesota. Keillor doctored the spelling a bit so that it better resembles a word from an indigenous North American language, where most of the North American lake and river names come from.

In addition to its beauty, *woebegone*'s age makes it slightly facetious. When we need to use *sad* or *sorrowful* with our tongue somewhere in our cheek, this good word is the perfect surrogate, "When someone took Natalie's parking space, she came in with such a woebegone expression on her face, you would have thought she had lost her best friend." Her car is such a woebegone old dinosaur, though, we are all surprised that she still drives it.

Today's word is an interesting example of a phrase reduced to a single word. In the thirteenth century people said things like, "Me has woe bigon." As the verb *bego* (*bewent, begone*) was slowly replaced by *beset*, *me* was replaced by *I*, keeping the sense of "I am beset by woe." By the fourteenth century the phrase had become an idiom, *I am woe begone*. Finally, in the course of the fifteenth century, the phrase became the single word that we enjoy today.

# Glossary

**Ablaut.** A peculiarity of Proto-Indo-European (for which see below) whereby all words containing an O in their root, have a correlate with an E, as in Greek pous, pod- "foot" and Latin pes, ped- "foot." No one knows what purpose ablaut served in Proto-Indo-European.

**Alliteration.** Consonant rhyme, the repetition of the same consonant, as in "Peter Piper picked a peck of pickled peppers."

**Antonym.** A word with the opposite meaning, as *black* is the antonym of *white*.

**Aphaeresis.** The loss of an initial vowel or syllable, as in the pronunciation of *opossum* as *'possum*.

**Assimilation.** A consonant becoming the same as or similar to the consonant next to it, as does the N in the Latin negative prefix *in-* in words like *irrelevant, immature*, and *illegal*.

**Blend.** The intentional creation of a word by smushing two words together, e.g. *smoke + fog > smog, motor + hotel > motel*.

**Case.** Noun and adjective case is a feature of the grammars of some languages whereby the function of a noun is indicated by a distinct ending on the noun. For example, while *tabula* means "board" in Latin, "of the board" is *tabulae*.

**Clipping.** The shortening of a word by removing a syllable or two from the end (*doc* for *doctor*), from the beginning (*van* for *caravan*) or from both ends (*flu* for *influenza*).

**Commonization.** The conversion of a proper noun into a common noun, as the name Boycott became the English verb *to boycott.*

**Count noun.** A noun referring to a countable object, e.g. *egg(s), basket(s), bike(s).* Count nouns, unsurprisingly, may be counted.

**Diminutive.** A form of a noun that refers to a small or beloved version of the noun's meaning, as *kitty* is a diminutive of *cat,* and *duckling* is a diminutive of *duck.* English no longer produces them but they are common in languages like German, Hebrew, and Russian.

**Eponym.** A proper noun that becomes commonized, as Charles C. Boycott (1832-1897) is the eponym of the verb *boycott.*

**Etymology.** The study of the history of words undertaken by etymologists.

**Euphemism.** An acceptable expression used in place of an unacceptable or taboo word, such as *pee* for the four-letter word, *Gee-whiz* for "Jesus," or *golly* for "God."

**Fickle N.** An N ([n] sound) that comes and goes in some Proto-Indo-European words for reasons we don't understand. We find it in the Latin infinitive frangere "to break" but not in the past participle fractus "broken."

**Fickle S.** An S ([s] sound) found at the beginning of some Proto-Indo-European words in some languages but not others, e.g. English *slack* comes from the same root as Latin *laxus* "lax."

**Folk etymology.** Reanalyzing a foreign word so that it is compatible with native words, as the foreign-sounding Spanish *cucaracha* was converted into *cockroach,* made up of two recognizable English words.

**Frequentative.** A special form of a verb that indicates that an action is repeated more than once.

**Indo-European.** Related to those languages of India except for the southern tip, Iran (Persian), Pakistan, Sri Lanka, the nonnative languages of the Americas, the European nations except for the Basque regions of Spain, Hungary, Turkey, Estonia, and Finland. The languages that developed from Proto-Indo-European (for which see below).

**Intransitive verb.** A verb that does not accept a direct object, a noun or noun phrase that refers to the thing on which the action of the verb is carried out. *Sleep* is an intransitive verb because we cannot sleep anything.

**Lexical.** Referring to words, vocabularies, and dictionaries.

**Linguistics.** The scientific study of language. A linguist is not necessarily a polyglot, someone who speaks more than one language, nor a translator. He is a psychologist who studies the structure of language and its behavior in the mind using scientific methods.

**Mass noun.** A noun referring to a substance or abstraction that cannot be counted, e.g. *contemplation, leisure, languor.* Mass nouns cannot be plural.

**Metathesis.** Two sounds switching places as in pronouncing *ask, aks,* or the pronunciation of *prescription* as *perscription.*

**Middle English.** English spoken from the middle of the twelfth century to about 1470.

**Modern English.** English as it is spoken today, since 1470.

**Old English.** The earliest form of English, spoken from the mid-fifth century to the mid-twelfth century in what is today England and Southern Scotland.

**Onomatopoeia.** The creation of a word that sounds like the sound it represents, e.g. *quack, meow, crack, slosh.*

**Participle.** A verb form that functions as an adjective. English has a present participle, e.g. *annoying* in the boy annoying the man, and a past participle, e.g. *annoyed,* in the man annoyed by the boy.

**Pejorative.** Having negative connotations.

**Proto-Indo-European (PIE).** An ancient language that probably existed about 5000 to 6000 years ago and from which all Indo-European languages later developed. There are no written records of the language. It has been reconstructed from the ancient and contemporary languages of India and Europe by comparing them to each other.

**Reduplication.** The repetition of a syllable that changes the meaning of a word, such as the repetition of the root *tin-* of tinnire "to ring" to produce tintinnare "to jingle."

**Rhotacism.** The conversion of an S to an R, as in Latin flos, florem "flower."

**Rhyming compound.** A compound made up of a word followed by a word that rhymes with it, such as *willy-nilly, namby-pamby, fuddy-duddy.*

**Synonym.** A word with the same meaning as another, as *couch* is a synonym of *sofa.*

**Transitive verb.** A verb that accepts a direct object, a noun or noun phrase that refers to the thing on which the action of the verb is carried out. *Bite* in the sentence, The man bit **the dog**, is a transitive verb because *the dog* is a direct object.

---

Keep an eye open for the next in Dr. Beard's series of best word books: *The 100 Sportiest Words in Sports.*

# Selected References

*American Heritage Dictionary of the English Language*. Boston: Houghton-Mifflin Publishers, 2000.

Chantrell, Glynnis. *The Oxford Dictionary of Word Histories*. Oxford: Oxford University Press, 2002.

*Encarta® World English Dictionary* [North American Edition]. http://encarta.msn.com/encnet/features/dictionary/dictionaryhome.aspx. Redmond, Washington: Microsoft, 2009.

*The Century Dictionary*, ed. William Dwight Whitney. Online: http://www.global-language.com/century. New York: Century Company, 1889.

Harper, Douglas. *Etymonline.com*. http://www.etymonline. com, 2001.

Klein, Ernest. *A Comprehensive Etymological Dictionary of the English Language*. Amsterdam: North Holland, 1966.

*Merriam-Webster Unabridged Dictionary*. Online: http://unabridged.merriam-webster.com. Springfield, Massachusetts: Merriam-Webster, 2009.

Pokorny, Julius. *Indogermanisches Etymologisches Wörterbuch*, 3rd ed. Tübingen-Basel: Franke Verlag, 1994.

*The Oxford English Dictionary*. Oxford: Oxford University Press, http://www.oed.com, 2008.

Skeat, Walter. *An Etymological Dictionary of the English Language*. Mineola, New York: Dover Publications, 2005.